A
Chorus
for
Peace

A Chorus for Peace

A GLOBAL
ANTHOLOGY
OF POETRY
BY WOMEN
Edited by
Marilyn Arnold,
Bonnie Ballif-Spanvill,
and Kristen Tracy

University of Iowa Press
Iowa City

University of Iowa Press, Iowa City 52242
Copyright © 2002 by the University of Iowa Press
All rights reserved
Printed in the United States of America
Design by Richard Hendel
http://www.uiowa.edu/~uipress

The publication of this book was generously
supported by the University of Iowa Foundation.

Printed on acid-free paper

Library of Congress
Cataloging-in-Publication Data
A chorus for peace: a global anthology of poetry by
women /edited by Marilyn Arnold, Bonnie Ballif-
Spanvill, and Kristen Tracy.
    p.   cm.
    Includes index.
    ISBN 0-87745-811-1 (cloth), ISBN 0-87745-812-x
(pbk.)
    1. Peace—Poetry. 2. Poetry—Women authors.
I. Arnold, Marilyn, 1935–. II. Ballif-Spanvill,
Bonnie, 1940–. III. Tracy, Kristen, 1972–.
PN6110.P4 C49 2002
808.81′0082—dc21   2002016009

02 03 04 05 06 C 5 4 3 2 1
02 03 04 05 06 P 5 4 3 2 1

To our daughters,

and their daughters,

and their daughters . . .

Contents

III. "WAR, AND SO FORTH"
     The Bitter Waste

IV. "NOW THAT I'M HELPLESS"
     Mothers in Ambiguity

v. "WHO STOPPED THE DANCE?"
   Domestic Battlefields

VI. "IT IS THE TIME OF AWAKENING"
    Reaching and Rebuilding

VII. "LISTEN FOR LIFE"
    Nature Speaks

VIII. "THE HEART HAS FOUND HOME"
    Peace to the Spirit

Acknowledgments

We express particular appreciation to Katie Marie Lenhard
for her untiring work in obtaining copyright permissions and
manuscript preparation. We also express appreciation to the
Women's Research Institute and to Clayne L. Pope, dean of the
College of Family, Home, and Social Sciences at Brigham Young
University, for their generous encouragement and support of this
project.

Introduction

The great humanitarian Albert Schweitzer made a profound statement in his *Memoirs of Childhood* that has particular application to this remarkable collection of poems by twentieth-century women from many nations of the world. This is what he said:

> All acts and facts are a product of spiritual power, the successful ones of power which is strong enough; the unsuccessful ones of power which is too weak. Does my behaviour in respect of love effect nothing? That is because there is not enough love in me. Am I powerless against the untruthfulness and the lies which have their being all around me? The reason is that I myself am not truthful enough. Have I to watch dislike and ill will carrying on their sad game? That means that I myself have not yet completely laid aside small-mindedness and envy. Is my love of peace misunderstood and scorned? That means that I am not yet sufficiently peace-loving.

What he suggests is that there is an inherent power in rightness, in goodness, in love, and in love of peace and that if even a single individual chooses to act rightly and truthfully and peacefully in the midst of tempting and contrary choices, the power of that act and aspiration can change the world. By extension, if untold numbers of single individuals love peace enough, seek peace enough, stand for peace enough, are themselves persons of peace, the ideal of peace will become the world's transforming reality.

The women whose poems appear in this collection stand for peace. Many of them have seen war and strife on fronts both international and domestic, and they write graphically and poignantly, and sometimes ironically, about conflicts external and internal that tear up lives. They write about the victims of war and oppression — bewildered and brutalized children, bereft wives and mothers, raped and mutilated women, tormented prisoners and soldiers. And they write about victims of a seemingly failed society and victims of struggling or failed human relationships — husbands and wives, parents and children, mothers and daughters, women trapped in demeaning roles, dangerous people with hopelessly twisted minds. But all the while, these writers are crying for peace, searching for peace, yearning for peace. Their cry is heard even when it is implied rather than uttered. And, yes, some, though not all, find peace—in relationships, in nature, in God, or deep inside themselves. In their search, in their desperate or merely quiet yearning, they are pointing the way for the rest of us.

Like Schweitzer, they declare that peace is a tangible power, a presence, something more than the absence of external conflict. They tell us that it is our task as women to give birth to peace out of the ashes of war and violence, and they insist that it can be done. Some portray only the anguish of turmoil, others offer just a glimpse of hopefulness, while others venture a full-blown vision of peace and harmony. Even as some of these poems expose our selfishness and our inhumanity, others reveal our generosity and our tenderness. From these poets, from the eloquent and varied voices who can articulate our human griefs and joys in ways we never could, we capture snatches of the dream of a peaceful society. If only for a moment, and sometimes by projecting its absence, these women envision a society free from want and anger, a society in which war is only a black scar on ancient memory, a society that has exchanged forgiveness for blame, love for violence, generosity for greed, healing for pain, reconciliation for antagonism, wholeness for fragmentation, togetherness for isolation, trust for suspicion, and faith for despair. They also envision a soul at peace with itself.

Just as some of these poems project images of destruction and pain, so others project images of beauty and light. In fact, the most recurrent images in the poems of hope and peace are the images of stars and birds—lofty, full of light, suggestive of a hallowed presence and a spiritual aspiration. There are also images of mirrors that, in holding together two disparate parts, suggest a reconciliation and restoration to wholeness. The poems run a full range of emotion—from the darkest pain to a flirtation with whimsy. What they suggest when taken together—and they do seem to form the parts of a larger whole, all-encompassing, all-comprehending—is the indomitability of the human spirit. As one writer puts it, "I am intact."

This collection, then, constitutes a chorus of gifted, global voices, all artists in their own right, all singing different parts, all bent on truth, all blending in a splendid and sometimes heart-breaking plea for peace. And, they seem to say, if women don't do this thing, if women don't make this world a peaceful place, who will? It appears to us, the preparers of this unique and stirring volume, that with the new millennium there is in the very air about us a renewed desire to create a society—a world—in which we return love for hate and selflessness for selfishness. And perhaps we are ready, at last, to become, each of us, the one who loves peace enough to make its power felt in every quarter of this earth.

The thoughtful reader might ask why the three of us envisioned such a volume, and why now? After all, war and violence are as old as the human race. We reply with our own question—why not now? Driven by our personal, and admittedly idealistic, dreams of a world at last done with hate and destruction, we find in the words of gifted women poets an expression of our deepest fears and our highest hopes. Perhaps women seem to speak most poignantly against violence because they, and the beloved children they have borne, are too often the helpless victims of that violence. We gathered these poems so voices too long muffled, too long ignored, could be heard together. As women ourselves, we feel our own vulnerability and shudder at the suffering of others. And as women, we want to join their impassioned cry for peace.

We have asked ourselves time and again, what perversity drives mortals to commit brutal acts against one another? Why are school-boys shooting their classmates? Why are fathers and mothers doing violence to their babies and to each other? Why does ambition drive ruthless leaders to make war? One small volume of poems is not going to change the world, we know that. But one small volume of poems might change a few hearts, might lead us one by one to become persons of conscience and disciples of peace. If an act of tenderness is multiplied by even fifty or a hundred, something important has begun.

The United Nations has proclaimed 2001–2010 the International Decade for a Culture of Peace and Nonviolence for the Children of the World. Women throughout the earth are crying out for an end to war and violence. In collecting their urgent pleas, we express through their eloquence our own compelling desire for

PART ONE

"Running from the Smoke"

CHILDREN IN WAR

War Photograph

A naked child is running
along the path toward us,
her arms stretched out,
her mouth open,
the world turned to trash
behind her.

She is running from the smoke
and the soldiers, from the bodies
of her mother and little sister
thrown down into a ditch,
from the blown-up bamboo hut
from the melted pots and pans.
And she is also running from the gods
who have changed the sky to fire
and puddled the earth with skin and blood.
She is running—my god—to us,
10,000 miles away,
reading the caption
beneath her picture
in a weekly magazine.
All over the country
we're feeling sorry for her
and being appalled at the war
being fought in the other world.
She keeps on running, you know,
after the shutter of the camera
clicks. She's running to us.
For how can she know,
her feet beating a path
on another continent?
How can she know
what we really are?
From the distance, we look
so terribly human.

The Choice

From a speech by Ellen Kuzwayo

The children who were shot in Johannesburg
for throwing stones didn't pick the stones up
in Johannesburg. There are no
stones there—not even pebbles. They
filled their pockets in Soweto
and walked all the way.

Teaching the Children

Children,
today we offer you
the holocaust.

Here are the bodies here
the bunkers here the young
who were the guards.

We offer to you
dear children
this package.

It may go off
in your hands if
you open it hastily

or later
if you set it
aside.

sorrow song

for the eyes of the children,
the last to melt,
the last to vaporize,
for the lingering
eyes of the children, staring,
the eyes of the children of
buchenwald,
of viet nam and johannesburg,
for the eyes of the children
of nagasaki,
for the eyes of the children
of middle passage,
for cherokee eyes, ethiopian eyes,
russian eyes, american eyes,
for all that remains of the children,
their eyes,
staring at us, amazed to see
the extraordinary evil in
ordinary men.

To Etan

An Israeli Child from the Kibbutz Ma'oz Hayim

He falls
under the star that branches
a wild tree in his hands
a web woven with the threads of steel stretching
       walls of blood
around The Dream.
He is caught.
Opening his eyes
Etan, the child, asks,
"How long do we have to watch over this land?"
And time deformed
dragged in khaki, bypasses him
through flames and smoke
sorrows and death.

If only the Star could foretell the truth.

Etan, my child
Like the harbor that is drowning
I can see you drown
through the lie
The bloated dream is a sinking load.
I am afraid for you, my child
to have to grow up in this web of things
to be gradually stripped of
       your human heart and face
you could fall again, my child
      and fall
        and fall
          fading into a fathomless end.

Translated by Kamal Boullata

Jerusalem

Let's be the same wound if we must bleed.
Let's fight side by side, even if the enemy
is ourselves: I am yours, you are mine.
  —*Tommy Olofsson, Sweden*

I'm not interested in
who suffered the most.
I'm interested in
people getting over it.

Once when my father was a boy
a stone hit him on the head.
Hair would never grow there.
Our fingers found the tender spot
and its riddle: the boy who has fallen
stands up. A bucket of pears
in his mother's doorway welcomes him home.
The pears are not crying.
Later his friend who threw the stone
says he was aiming at a bird.
And my father starts growing wings.

Each carries a tender spot:
something our lives forgot to give us.
A man builds a house and says,
"I am native now."
A woman speaks to a tree in place
of her son. And olives come.
A child's poem says,
"I don't like wars,
they end up with monuments."
He's painting a bird with wings
wide enough to cover two roofs at once.

Why are we so monumentally slow?
Soldiers stalk a pharmacy:
big guns, little pills.
If you tilt your head just slightly
it's ridiculous.

There's a place in my brain
where hate won't grow.
I touch its riddle: wind, and seeds.
Something pokes us as we sleep.

It's late but everything comes next.

Bread and Water

After the Leningrad trials, after solitary confinement
most of eleven years in a Siberian Gulag, he told us
this story. One slice of sour black bread a day.
He trimmed off the crust and saved it for the last
since it was the best part. Crunchy, even a little sweet.
Then he crumbled the slice into tiny pieces. And ate
them, one crumb at a time. So they lasted all day. Not
the cup of hot water. First he warmed his hands around it.
Then he rubbed the cup up and down his chest to warm his
body. And drank it fast. Why, we asked him, why not
like the bread? Sometimes, he said, there was more hot
water in the jug the guard wheeled around to the prisoners.
Sometimes a guard would ladle a second cup. It helped
to believe in such kindness.

The Lamb

It was a picture I had after the war.
A bombed English church. I was too young
to know the word *English* or *war*,
but I knew the picture.
The ruined city still seemed noble.
The cathedral with its roof blown off
was not less godly. The church was the same
plus rain and sky. Birds flew in and out
of the holes God's fist made in the walls.
All our desire for love or children
is treated like rags by the enemy.
I knew so much and sang anyway.
Like a bird who will sing until
it is brought down. When they take
away the trees, the child picks up a stick
and says, this is a tree, this the house
and the family. As we might. Through a door
of what had been a house, into the field
of rubble, walks a single lamb, tilting
its head, curious, unafraid, hungry.

Rain at Noon-time

For Julius Nyerere

a feastful sight
you see them now our people
this noon of leavening shadows
come sit round together to
dance the dance of children . . .

you say . . .

dance the dance of rippling waters
as now our history gathers
the foliage hold their palms to the skies
faces frowning look up to the skies
in our lands where laughter weeps unknowing

dance with us a dance of the future
they will not let us sit in peace
nor let our eyelids droop in earned rest
and the flood comes that must

they will not let the raindrops say
rain time is peace time
for the bursting forth of joys.

Myriad Stars, Part 132

My heart,
Yesterday you told me
  The world is joyful,
Yet today you tell me
  The world is disappointing.
What will
  Your words be tomorrow?
How can I believe you!

Translated by Michelle Yeh

[Suddenly]

Suddenly,
rising from my breast
hidden to protect me
from tear gas:
the smell of lemon.

Translated by Leza Lowitz, Miyuki Aoyama, and Akemi Tomioka

PART TWO

"On the Sidewalks of Love and Fire"

WOMEN SURVIVING WAR

When I Was Prettiest in My Life

When I was prettiest in my life,
the cities crumbled down,
and the blue sky appeared
in the most unexpected places.

When I was prettiest in my life,
a lot of people around me were killed,
in factories, in the sea, and on nameless islands.
I lost the chance to dress up like a girl should.

When I was prettiest in my life,
no men offered me thoughtful gifts.
They only knew how to salute in the military fashion.
They all went off to the front, leaving their beautiful eyes
    behind.

When I was prettiest in my life,
my head was empty,
my heart was obstinate,
and only my limbs had the bright color of chestnuts.

When I was prettiest in my life,
my country lost in a war.
"How can it be true?" I asked,
striding, with my sleeves rolled up, through the prideless town.

When I was prettiest in my life,
jazz music streamed from the radio.
Feeling dizzy, as if I'd broken a resolve to quit smoking,
I devoured the sweet music of a foreign land.

When I was prettiest in my life,
I was most unhappy,
I was most absurd,
I was helplessly lonely.

Therefore I decided to live a long time, if I could,
like old Rouault of France,
who painted magnificent pictures in his old age.

Translated by Edward Lueders and Naoshi Koriyama

For My Torturer, Lieutenant D . . .

You slapped me—
  no one had ever slapped me—
electric shock
and then your fist
and your filthy language
I bled too much to be able to blush
All night long
a locomotive in my belly
rainbows before my eyes
It was as if I were eating my mouth
drowning my eyes
I had hands all over me
and felt like smiling.

Then one morning a different soldier came
You were as alike as two drops of blood.
Your wife, Lieutenant—
Did she stir the sugar in your coffee?
Did your mother dare to tell you you looked well?
Did you run your fingers through your kids' hair?

Translated by Anita Barrows

Rwanda

My neighbor used to come to our hut,
bringing melons so sweet
I thought I should not eat them,
because I would die
and haunt my family like a ghost
with hard, black seeds for eyes.
One day, he brought his uncle and two friends
and they asked my father to go outside with them.
I thought he had come to get permission to marry me
and I was glad because I loved him,
even though he wasn't a member of my tribe,
nor as educated as I was.
I wanted to stay,
but my mother gave me a basket of clothes
to wash at the river.
She said, "Don't come back,
until they are as clean as the Virgin Mary's soul."
"Mother," I said, "I'll never come back then."
"Shall I take my brother?" I asked,
as he ran to my father's side.
I was laughing, when she hissed, "Run,"
and I did because she frightened me.
As I rounded the hut,
I heard the *tat, tat, tat,* from guns
like the ones the soldiers carry.
I ran faster, still holding the basket.
It was frozen to my hands
and I still held it, even as I jumped in the river.
I thought I would die, so I closed my eyes.
When something bumped against me,
I opened them and saw my father's body.
As he floated past me,
his arm hooked around my neck,
almost taking me under

and I released the basket.
I reached for my father, as bullets hit the water
and I dove under him.
His body shielded me, until I couldn't breathe
and had to break the surface for air.
When I crawled onto the riverbank,
I hid in the grass behind the church.
Finally, when I was sure no one was around,
I beat on the rectory door,
until the priest opened it. "Hide me, Father," I begged.
Once inside, I was overjoyed to see my mother.
She told me when my neighbor shot at her,
she pretended to be dead
and while he dumped my father in the river,
she escaped and came here,
hoping I had survived.
She said we needed another place to hide,
but she could only find a small closet-size space
behind the altar, covered by a sheet of tin.
Only one of us could fit, so she made me go in
and covered the hole again.
When I heard screaming, I kicked the tin aside
and saw my mother was on fire.
I tried to help her, using only my hands,
but when she was completely covered in flames,
I broke a stained-glass window
with a statue of Saint Joseph and climbed out.
As I crawled back to the river,
a shiver of wind passed over me
through the grass and trees.
When I stopped to rest,
fear coiled around me like a snake,
but when I told myself I would not let them kill me,
it took the shape of a bird and flew away.
I crawled back to the church,
because I wanted to find my mother's ashes,
so I could bury them,
but my way was blocked by the rebels,

so I waited until dark.
Maybe I slept. I don't know.
When I heard my neighbor's voice,
it was as if I had awakened from a dream.
Relief flooded over me, until I sat up
and saw him standing above me, holding a machete.
"Sister," he said, "I won't hurt you."
I knew he was lying and I tried to get away,
but I was too weak
and he fell on top of me, tearing at my clothes.
When he was finished raping me,
I thought he would kill me,
but he only brought the machete close to my head,
then let it fall from his hands.
Dawn had come to the village
with more killing on its mind.
I heard screams and pleas for mercy,
then I realized those sounds were inside me.
They would never leave.
Now I am always talking to the dead.
Their bones are rattling around in my head.
Sometimes I can't hear anything else
and I go to the river with my son and cry.
When he was a few days old,
I took him there for the first time.
I stood looking at the water,
which was still the color of blood,
then I lifted him high above my head,
but my mother's bones said, "Killing is a sin,"
so I took him home
to raise him as if he really is my son
and not the issue of my neighbor,
who has returned to torment me
with skin that smells like burning flesh,
but in my heart I know
both his mother and father died long ago
and left this orphan to grow like a poisoned flower
beside the open grave that was my country.

[Eternally to be waiting for bloody news]

Eternally to be waiting for bloody news,
to bring up children in a whisper,
to hide manuscripts under a diaper.
Who's the informer? is our main secret.
Who comes to the house when we're not there?
Who's that making a tape go round in the telephone?
How many years d'you get for this, how many winters?
Down what slope do we slide,
if we've drunk a glass of tea with a foreigner?
How not to avoid catching the eye
of people you must not give your hand to
if you're still not a complete shit?
How can we be absent everywhere?
Hide and breathe in water
with gills? For how many days, moments,
anticipating the worst, to flee?
And where to? And must we give birth
to so many generations for the prison?

Translated by Gerald S. Smith

I Remember Haifa Being Lovely But

there were snakes in the
tent, my mother was
strong but she never
slept, was afraid of
dreaming. In Auschwitz
there was a numbness,
lull of just staying
alive. Her two babies
gassed before her, Dr.
Mengele, you know who
he is? She kept her
young sister alive
only to have her die
in her arms the night
of liberation. My mother
is big boned, but she
weighed under 80 lbs.
It was hot, I thought
the snakes lovely. No
drugs in Israel, no
food. I got pneumonia,
my mother knocked the
doctor to the floor
when they refused,
said I lost two in
the camp and if this
one dies I'll kill
myself in front of
you. I thought that
once you became a
mother, blue numbers
appeared mysteriously,
tattooed on your arm

The Night before Good-bye

Mama is mending
my underwear
while my brothers sleep.
Her husband taken away by the FBI
one son lured away by the Army
now another son and daughter
lusting for the free world outside.
She must let go.
The war goes on.
She will take one still small son
and join Papa in internment
to make a family.
Still sewing
squinting in the dim light
in room C barrack 4 block 4
she whispers
Remember
keep your underwear
in good repair
in case of accident
don't bring shame
on us.

Demonstration

The tire burns in an empty square.
One child, pockets filled with
Carefully collected stones,
Stares at the army patrol.

At his funeral we chanted
"Mother of the martyr rejoice,
All youths are your children."

Translated by Kamal Boullata

[When she showed me her photograph]

When she showed me her photograph
she said,
This is my daughter.
She still hasn't come home.
She hasn't come home in ten years.
But this is her photograph.
Isn't it true that she is very pretty?
She is a philosophy student
and here she is when she was
fourteen years old
and had her first
communion,
starched, sacred.
This is my daughter.
She is so pretty.
I talk to her every day.
She no longer comes home late, and this is why I reproach
    her much less.
But I love her so much.
This is my daughter.
Every night I say goodbye to her.
I kiss her
and it's hard for me not to cry
even though I know she will not come
home late
because as you know, she has not come
home for years.
I love this photo very much.
I look at it every day.
It seems that only yesterday
she was a little feathered angel in my arms
and here she looks like a young lady,
a philosophy student,
another disappeared.

But isn't it true that she is so pretty,
that she has an angel's face,
that it seems as if she were still alive?

Translated by Celeste Kostopulos-Cooperman

In the Casbah

I thought the War was . . .
here we died, Mai and I,
flattened by armored wheels
while you were fooling around
    in the Casbah . . .
I found my children's broken bodies
lying in the streets and picked them up,
I swam over my head in nightmare,
then they yanked off my skin,
hung it over flame to dry
and once more I almost drowned
    in their dream.
I flew, crawled, hid—
I heard the wind crying:
    "Salma . . . Salma
they've bought and sold you"
thousand snakes a blazing coil
    around my heart.
And you were fooling around
    in the Casbah,
        weren't you,
when our nation became
war's killing ground?

Translated by Charles Doria

Midnight

Midnight. The flowing water of Hu T'o River
Sounds more distinctly.
Suddenly a strong wind blows.
The wind's sound and the water's sound
Together become an enormous roar.
I cannot sleep in peace.
The voices of nature speak
To the troubled hearts of men.
I lie quietly, stilling my heart.
I refuse to remember
The tragic death of the father of my sons.
I refuse to remember
The husband and wife
Embracing, leaning against each other,
Or the sons and daughters around their knees.
I will not imagine
My youngest son's fate on the battlefield.
With all my heart I long for the dawn.
The cruelty of Fascism
The violence and corruption of the enemy
Have turned white the hair of mothers
And wrinkled their foreheads.
At last the dawn comes.
But with it come again
Savage battles, young men falling,
Others taking their places
In heroic sacrifice.
How many of my friends
Are already mothers of martyrs?
Perhaps I am one of them.

Translated by Kenneth Rexroth and Ling Chung

Plaza de Mayo

Every Thursday, every Thursday
Mr. General
I curl my hair
put on lipstick
to meet friendship and pain
at the Plaza de Mayo.

Every Thursday, every Thursday
Mr. General
I put on my party dress
to meet torture and hatred
at the Plaza de Mayo.

My son was young
black-haired and happy
Mr. General
But now long-eyed fish
deep in the River Plate
eat his body
bite by bite.

My hair, my hair
Mr. General
however much I tie it up
comes loose like snakes
and stands on end to the sky.

My shoes, my shoes
Mr. General
walk by themselves
in the dark street of terror.

My daughter was tall, blond, inquisitive
Mr. General
she raised her thin arm against you

they seized her, beat her, raped her
now I don't know whether she is alive or dead
but I hear her calling
with a cold and aqueous voice.

Every Thursday, every Thursday
Mr. General
I put on a belt of love
to meet death
in the circle of women-mothers
at the Plaza de Mayo.

I ate salt poison powerlessness
Mr. General
I drank hatred terror and loss
my son was beautiful and happy
Mr. General
my daughter tall and sincere.

I don't wish you death
Mr. General
death is such a little thing
something sweet and gentle

I don't want revenge
Mr. General
revenge saturates and weakens
it only satisfies the sick sex.

I don't wish you pain
Mr. General
pain purifies the heart
it makes it fly through the window
like my son's heart did.

I want the kind of love that creates love
I want desire that incites desires
I want life that creates life

I don't want mothers to give birth
to innocent and peaceful children
that later turn into tyrants, torturers,
and Generals like you
Mr. General.

Translated by Gail Wronsky

Mother's Inheritance

Mother,
You did not leave me an inheritance of
     necklaces for a wedding
but a neck
   that towers above the guillotine
Not an embroidered veil for my face
but the eyes of a falcon
   that glitter like the daggers
   in the belts of our men.
Not a piece of land large enough
   to plant a single date palm
but the primal fruit of The Fertile Crescent:
My Womb.

You let me sleep with all the children
   of our neighborhood
that my agony may give birth
   to new rebels

In the bundle of your will
I thought I could find
   a seed from The Garden of Eden
   that I may plant in my heart
   forsaken by the seasons
Instead
You left me with a sheathless sword
   the name of an obscure child carved on its blade
Every pore in me
   every crack
   opened up:
A sheath.

I plunged the sword into my heart
   but the wall could not contain it

I thrust it into my lungs
   but the window could not box it
I dipped it into my waist
   but the house was too small for it
It lengthened into the streets
   defoliating the decorations
   of official holidays
Tilling asphalt
Announcing the season of
The Coming Feast.

Mother,
Today, they came to confiscate the inheritance
   you left me.
They could not decipher the children's fingerprints
They could not walk the road that stretches
   between the arteries of my heart
   and the cord that feeds the babe
   in every mother's womb.
They seized the children of the neighborhood
   for interrogation
They could not convict the innocence in their eyes.
They searched my pockets
   took off my clothes
   peeled my skin
But they failed to reach
   the glistening silk that nestles
   the twin doves
   in my breast.

Translated by Kamal Boullata

Gone Are Those We Love

To Kamal Naser, Yusef Najjar, and Kamal "Adwan"

One eagle after another
vanished into darkness.
One by one they were
slain
for having towered above the clouds.
Motherland
for your sake
their blood was spilled
like rosary beads of rubies slip.
Gone are those we love.

Sorrow had no voice, behold
Sorrow flowers silence to my lips
and words
fall
much the same as their bodies fell
        corpses
     distorted.
   what else could I say?
their blood is smearing
my vision.
Gone are those we love.

Before their vessel ever anchored
before their eyes ever caught sight of
the distant port.

Palestine
in the seasons of your irremediable mourning
you drank cups of absinthe we drank
your thirst was unquenched
ours eternal.
Waterless we shall remain

here at the mouth of this fountain
till the day of their return
with the ocean of dawns that they embraced:
    A vision that knows no death.
    A love that has no end.

Translated by Kamal Boullata

Women

They were women then
My mama's generation
Husky of voice—Stout of
Step
With fists as well as
Hands
How they battered down
Doors
And ironed
Starched white
Shirts
How they led
Armies
Headragged Generals
Across mined
Fields
Booby-trapped
Ditches
To discover books
Desks
A place for us
How they knew what we
Must know
Without knowing a page
Of it
Themselves.

JUDITH STRASSER

Memory Lapse

For an older friend

I am prepared when you don't show up. For three days
and three nights, I have been watching
the War in the Gulf. I baked a cake while we bombed
Baghdad. I set the table; they shelled Tel Aviv.
You are like one of the casualties. All fall,
during the build-up, panic rattled the telephone lines.
You boiled pots dry, missed appointments, lost
your wallet, your checkbook, your keys. You made
company meals for guests you did not invite.
We worried the facts to shreds: drug interactions,
Jack Daniel's blackouts, Alzheimer's disease.

The commercials come back. I run to the kitchen
to turn off the coffee pot. The calendar on the wall
targets your visit in red: 1:00 P.M. Saturday, next week.
I see the error is mine. I didn't expect the shock
of war. I didn't think of battle fatigue.
I never considered grief.

Don't Think Governments End the World

Don't think governments end the world. The blast,
the burnings, and the final famine will
be brought on *by mistake*. "I'm sorry," the last
anxious man at the control panel will
try to say, his face streaked with panic, red
hives rising on his neck. He'll have been a jerk
all his life, who couldn't get through his head
that his mother couldn't love him. Work
at the panel would give him the control
that she had denied him again and again.

Thus the world will burn through the central hole
of his being. He won't really be sure—again,
having never been assured of her—of what
he is supposed to do. That is, he'll be sure
at every exercise until the shut
blank door of the final moment injures
his gerrybuilt control and BANG, BANG, BANG.

It won't be his fault, his childish mother's fault,
or the fault of what produced her or what
produced what produced her back through the vault
of savage centuries. If he'd just known what,
he'd have done it to please. He might have known himself
through what he'd felt, and thus might be clear.
She might have said, "That's nice, dear,"
and we wouldn't be dead.

Aren't you scared of your life in his hands?
But of all the men whose hands you'd hope to be in,
name the one you're sure of. The history of nations
is cold; the world burns by generations.

Do Not Throw Away

Do not throw away
That scoop of passion from the past.
Even though passion flows softly like water
At the bottom of a cool mountain spring
In a pine grove on a dark night
And sighs an elusive sigh,
You must still preserve that truth.
The moon is still bright;
The lights below the hills are still on;
The sky is still full of stars
Hanging like dreams.
You ask the night for
Those words back—you must still believe
Their echoes
In the valley.

Translated by Michelle Yeh

Lament

Those we love die like birds
mourned by orange trees which never wither
tomorrow when birds return to Ghaza
to peck at your blue window
while narcissus perfume is everywhere
and jasmine fills the air
the henna tree will still stand
alone, a stranger to the world

On dark alley walls
our comrades' deaths are announced
posters show their smiling faces
The usual way we learn
one has fallen on the long road
We discovered in blood's path
        that death is life continuance
life deeply rooted in death
Yet when they drank to you in the pine woods
I asked why
        a tear hesitated in my cousin's eye
the tear in her green eye
that told me of your death
        what a great poster that'll make!

I burn with grief
I am no stone
yearning is a burden
for you bridge my life and death.
On Omar al-Mukhtar Street
foreign helmets that sting like whips
block your funeral
pursuing your beloved name
wrapped in a coffin that rests on Ghaza's wounds
        . . . .

I am no stone
you fighter up to the moment of bitter death
whose perfume time after time rained down
            from your window
penetrating you three times
on the fourth time you fell
dissolving all memories in my blood
floating on the tree-lined road to the old graveyard
where the grass laughed at my childhood's shadow
            and accompanied me to your resting place
            .   .   .   .

I am no stone
so I welcome your magic footsteps
            when they come
joy pours from my bosom
all doors open in my face
I blame myself
I pledge you will be my eternal shadow
            .   .   .   .

Did they kill you?
Your wounds pierce every city
            that lies dreaming in the summer
Trees bleed, bird wings break
            the scent of basil everywhere
            in the alleys
            although passers-by
            do not even notice you
don't they know your name is hunted?
    That you are under siege?
            .   .   .   .

I am no stone
is it because blood's gleam
is all that's hopeful in the world that
we write our own histories
draw our faces' features in it

fix our seal
on the brows of the motherland
   we love so well
building it anew?

In blood we appoint the time
   to sow
   for it is the secret to freshness
Is it because we refuse to multiply like weeds or seagrass
  that lack identity or form
  to define our origin
tears dance from me
my joy weeps
joy that stretches to include
the last arm hurling death
at the aggressor's patrol
that stalk your streets
   which God has forsaken?

      . . . .

Time never ends its moments
the pride of your grief purifies
all moments passing through
the mind of the stars
and the veins of the stones
No bullet will pass
   without changing faces in some new way

Time will never end
for you are a beginning that never ceases
all about you the strangeness of things vanishes
they enjoy again the innocence of their first beginnings
I learn to perfection the art of waiting
   on the sidewalks of love and fire

Translated by Charles Doria with the help of Salma al-Khadra'
al-Jayyusi

A Mother

The mother in the green sweater walks and walks along the
    street.
In Elul, the wind swings,
Tebeth snows,
Pesach leaks sun over windowpanes.
The green sweater walks and walks along the street,
Through summers,
Through winters,
Through so much time.
The streets swim lengthwise and aslant,
The sky swings like a hammock,
And all the streets,
All lead to Pawiak.
There, like a wound, a prison cell burns,
A cell sways day and night;
Beneath the gray walls a daughter sits closed,
Locked,
Silent,
With folded hands,
With keen hearing,
And saws the bars with her gaze
And counts the stars.
Around her, the silence resounds,
The vacancy dazzles with white spears.
—
—
—

The green sweater walks and walks along the street.
Elul is not damp,
And Tebeth is not cold,
And Pesach is not a holiday.
The sky swings like a hammock,
And all the streets,
All lead to Pawiak.

Translated by Kathryn Hellerstein

To *El Mingo* (with Whom I Share Eva Victoria and Anahi Paz)

Of victory what remains for us is just
the name of our daughter,
emblazoned,
written under the bitter shadow
of those *compañeros*
who didn't reach defeat
with blood in their bodies.
And of peace, my love, what remains for us
is just the name of our daughter
among doves
and the memory of the dream of the bullet
in the center of the forehead
of the assassin.
Of justice

Translated by Gail Wronsky

Freedom Child — Tilla's Lullaby

And as I rock you
gently
I will sing.
I will sing to you
of skies dawning
to the bright lights —
of hope.
I will lull
I will lull
your slumber
not to the hollow
sounding thuds
of lash
on raw black flesh,
not to the clank
of chains,
but to a roar
from throats
sounding freedom.
Sound freedom
into the ears
of generations,
pile edifices
to deeper freedom
truer freedom.

Sound freedom
won by Ogun's
reddened machetes
sound freedom
won in war
in subterfuge.
And I will soothe
I will soothe

your sleep
with tales
of Toussaint, Dessalines
Cuffy, Cudjoe
Nanny and Boukman

I will show you
your ancestors
labelled warrior
and not victim.
I will teach you
a history of resistance.
Suck from my breasts
the will
to fight
the strength to
hope.

Suck from my breasts
my love.
It is a season
to bind
in
love

It is a season
to sow seed
plant fruit
spawn fruit
spawn nations
I will sing . . .
sing to you of
freedom

PART THREE

"War, and so Forth"

THE BITTER WASTE

[Lit up]

Lit up
from the side of death,
life may not
always be
shining and crimson.

Translated by Leza Lowitz, Miyuki Aoyama, and Akemi Tomioka

The Century's Decline

Our twentieth century was going to improve on the others.
It will never prove it now,
now that its years are numbered,
its gait is shaky,
its breath is short.

Too many things have happened
that weren't supposed to happen,
and what was supposed to come about
has not.

Happiness and spring, among other things,
were supposed to be getting closer.

Fear was expected to leave the mountains and the valleys.
Truth was supposed to hit home
before a lie.

A couple of problems weren't going
to come up anymore:
hunger, for example,
and war, and so forth.

There was going to be respect
for helpless people's helplessness,
trust, that kind of stuff.

Anyone who planned to enjoy the world
is now faced
with a hopeless task.

Stupidity isn't funny.
Wisdom isn't gay.
Hope
isn't that young girl anymore,
et cetera, alas.

God was finally going to believe
in a man both good and strong,
but good and strong
are still two different men.

"How should we live?" someone asked me in a letter.
I had meant to ask him
the same question.

Again, and as ever,
as may be seen above,
the most pressing questions
are naïve ones.

Translated by Stanisław Barańczak and Clare Cavanagh

I Had a Strange Dream

I had a strange dream last night:
I was to be shot at dawn.
I was imprisoned in a concrete basement
From which the dawn was not visible.
And then one of my classmates appeared,
We used to sit together at the same desk,
Copying out exercises from each other
And throwing a paper dart
(For some reason it wouldn't fly).
My classmate said: "Good evening.
How unlucky you've been. I'm very sorry.
I mean, being shot—it's so inhumane.
I've always believed in soft measures.
But somehow no one asked me,
They just gave me a pistol and sent me.
I'm not here alone, you know, my family's here,
I've got a wife and kids—a son and daughter.
Look, I can show you their photographs.
My daughter's like me, don't you think?
You see, I've got an old mother.
I mustn't put her health at risk.
The council gave us a new flat just recently,
It's got a pink-tiled bathroom.
And my wife wants a washing machine.
I mean, I can't . . . Anyway, it's no good . . .
There's nothing we can do to change things.
I've a pass to go to the Crimea, to a sanatorium.
They'll shoot you at dawn all the same.
If they hadn't sent me, it'd have been another.
Perhaps somebody you didn't know.
And after all we did go to school together.
And throw paper darts together.
You've just no idea how bad
It makes me feel, but what can you do?"

Translated by David McDuff

Women Don't Die on the Front Lines

Women don't die on the front lines
their heads don't roll like golf balls,
they don't sleep under a rain forest of gunpowder,
they don't leave the sky in ruins.
No snow freezes in their hearts.
Women don't die on the front lines,
they don't drive the devil out of Jerusalem
they don't blow up aqueducts or railroads,
they don't master the arts of war,
or of peace, either.
They don't make generals
or unknown soldiers carved out of stone
in town squares.
Women don't die on the front lines.
They are statues of salt in the Louvre,
mothers like Phaedra,
lovers of Henry the Eighth,
Mata Haris,
Eva Perons,
queens counselled by Prime Ministers,
nursemaids, cooks, washerwomen,
romantic poets.
Women don't make history,
but at nine months they push it out of their bellies
then sleep for twenty-four hours
like a soldier on leave from the front.

Translated by Pamela Carmell

September 11, 1973

Santiago, Chile

We shall overcome!
I heard at eight
we shall overcome!
I heard again
at nine

and at ten
and at eleven
and all
the hours
in the petrified day

after

the voices

lowered

weakened

folded

and the silence

devoured the echo

echo
   echo
echo
   echo
echo
   echo

without me realizing
it became
the sound
of bullets
against the body
of those who rose in opposition

No

No,
no
not
numbers.
They are not numbers.

They are names.

Nocturnal Visits

I think of our anonymous boys
of our burnt-out heroes
the amputated
the cripples
those who lost both legs
both eyes
the stammering teenagers.
At night I listen to their phantoms
shouting in my ear
shaking me out of lethargy
issuing me commands
I think of their tattered lives
of their feverish hands
reaching out to seize ours.
It's not that they're begging
they're demanding
they've earned the right to order us
to break up our sleep
to come awake
to shake off once and for all
this lassitude.

Translated by D. J. Flakoll

Every Day

War is no longer declared,
but simply continued. The unheard of
has become the everyday. The hero
keeps clear of battles. The weak
are pushed to the front-lines.
The uniform of the day is patience,
the decoration the paltry star
of hope above the heart.

It's awarded
when nothing more happens,
when drum-fire ceases,
when the enemy becomes invisible
and the shadow of eternal armament
covers the sky.

It's awarded
for desertion of flags,
for courage in the face of the friend,
for betraying unworthy secrets
and disregard
of every command.

Translated by Daniel Huws

Naturalization Papers

We daughters of foreign women
were born with minute compasses.
In nobler days
we visited Parisian museums.
We went into the Louvre in search of the Gioconda.
We too grew up amid adversity
and smiled predictable smiles.
If the war blew us out of the Old World,
a gust of wind condemns us to double vision.
We'll remain for perpetuity.
Torn between staying and leaving,
we'd like to give birth to storms,
so our blood will fall on terra firma
till our roots are lost in history.

Translated by Cynthia Steele

Judgement

My poems are all jagged at the edges
because I am a woman
who is jagged at the edges
I speak only of what I know.

Our memories are like broken glass
rubbing over smooth skin
the glass pierces the skin
and splinters there
blood oozes out and gives birth
to a cry: long and silent,
a cry for justice.
It shatters the universe.

Our memories are like jagged glass
they betray you
they speak of racism,
torture, deliberate genocide and rape.

This is our hell
but yours is the next.

The white leopard shall stalk the streets
devouring everything in its path
even the hand that spawned it.

People will run before it falling
amid the stench of rotting flesh.
We shall fall and disappear
but the earth shall refuse
to accept your carcass.

This is *your* nightmare.

Shame Shame
everybody knows
your name
and your crime

I am a woman
jagged at the edges
no longer able to forgive
I speak only of what I know
I know the universe
moves in a circle
so that your deeds
will find you.

Destiny

We kill what we love. What's left
was never alive.
No one else is so close. What is forgotten,
what is absent or less, hurts no one else.
We kill what we love. Enough of drawing a choked breath
through someone else's lung!
There is not air enough
for both of us. And the earth will not hold
both our bodies
and our ration of hope is small
and pain cannot be shared.

Man is an animal of solitudes,
a deer that bleeds as it flees
with an arrow in its side.

Ah, but hatred with its insomniac
glass eyes; its attitude
of menace and repose.

The deer goes to drink and a tiger
is reflected in the water.

The deer drinks the water and the image. And becomes
—before he is devoured—(accomplice, fascinated)
his enemy.

We give life only to what we hate.

Translated by Magda Bogin

[This is sung at dawn]

This is sung at dawn
of tomorrow's morning,
on the trampled ashes
of love that seemed to be.

This is sung with a chill,
as if it's not hard
to light a bonfire in secret
and trample it in public.

This is sung any old how,
not trying to be in tune,
as if life had been a trifle,
not a burnt-out place.

Translated by Gerald S. Smith

Air Raid

When people were being killed
how could the sky have been so beautiful?

I had never seen such a gorgeous sunset.
Even the clouds were going up in flames.

When I crawled out of the shelter
a fragment of the night sky hissed obliquely by my ears.
Overwhelming light flared in eight glass windows,
one color fighting against another,
all reflected sumptuously as on a screen —

the red struggling to redeem
the blue of day from the black sky,
purple looming, green dashing, orange flowing,
colors of all kinds mixing, shrieking —

was it the southern part of the city
that was bathing in golden rain
falling brightly, god knows from where?
Was it an alien world enclosed within the glass?
Was it silent, dark, heated air
that whirled about, encircling
the dumbfounded little Nero?

How could a war have been
so beautiful?

Translated by Edward Lueders and Naoshi Koriyama

The End and the Beginning

After every war
someone has to tidy up.
Things won't pick
themselves up, after all.

Someone has to shove
the rubble to the roadsides
so the carts loaded with corpses
can get by.

Someone has to trudge
through sludge and ashes,
through the sofa springs,
the shards of glass,
the bloody rags.

Someone has to lug the post
to prop the wall,
someone has to glaze the window,
set the door in its frame.

No sound bites, no photo opportunities,
and it takes years.
All the cameras have gone
to other wars.

The bridges need to be rebuilt,
the railroad stations, too.
Shirtsleeves will be rolled
to shreds.

Someone, broom in hand,
still remembers how it was.
Someone else listens, nodding

his unshattered head.
But others are bound to be bustling nearby
who'll find all that
a little boring.

From time to time someone still must
dig up a rusted argument
from underneath a bush
and haul it off to the dump.

Those who knew
what this was all about
must make way for those
who know little.
And less than that.
And at last nothing less than nothing.

Someone has to lie there
in the grass that covers up
the causes and effects
with a cornstalk in his teeth,
gawking at clouds.

Translated by Stanisław Barańczak and Clare Cavanagh

[And, having started singing this melody]

And, having started singing this melody,
we didn't compose a refrain for it,
and when we were led out to be shot,
we didn't feel like it any longer,
we stood under the wall, breaking into a sweat,
and the wall started sweating after us,
and the trembling misty dawn
lit up someone else's triumph.

But this melody went up
like a rainbow against the gray vault of the sky,
like a stalk breaking through asphalt,
like a shower one forgetful Thursday,
and the bullet rolled down out of the barrel
like a huge teardrop about freedom,
and the souls rushed out of our ribs
bouncing like a five-kopek piece, upward.

Translated by Gerald S. Smith

Season of Beginning and End

Behind the gate of light,
the lady of the languishing moon,
of the echoes,
of vanishing dew,
rests.

Shall we begin at zero point?
What harm in that?
The season of creation begins in the
season of nothingness:
    the arduous climb
    is the beginning of the end.

Behind the gate of light the lady
of the quiescent moon
of the vanishing sunset watches
the snows about to melt while
moonrays drown in the mirror.

Show me a place where I could
lie quietly among corners
a jungle where I can take shade,
a flower whose dew and fragrance I can breathe.
Grass loves all depths and distances,
but is also found in the surface
of the road that contains it.

The desert sun flirted with the clouds
in the hall of silence, or of those thirsty sands;
nothingness delivered the blow of death.
What harm to repeat the story?

What harm to us?
The season of creation begins in
the season of nothingness
if it is tended carefully.

But
by climbing,
one reaches the top of the slope.
Shall we begin?
Or is this
the beginning of the end?

*Translated by Patricia Alanah Byrne with the help
of Salma al-Khadra' al-Jayyusi*

There Is No Hope

There is no hope
that things will work out
that the pain will let up
and the world settle down.
It's not at all clear that
life will sort out
its chaotic dimensions
its mindless gestures.
There will be no happy end
no kiss everlasting
of rapt surrender
to herald other days.
Nor will there be any
early spring morning
fresh and fragrant
to set out lighthearted.
Instead all the pain
will invade anew
and nothing will be spared
its heavy stain.
We'll have to go on
keep right on breathing
put up with the light
and vilify sleep
cook with no faith
mate with no passion
chew with distaste
forever after with no tears.

Translated by Louise Popkin

Here I Am Once More . . .

Here I am once more before the sea
smashing whole doors against the rocks
mingling in the same bitter rolling motion
sand and pearls
in the burning metallic waves
the jasmine of my childhood and the shriek-owl of hell.

Here I am once more before the sea, bent over
under the annual booty of rancour
of fatigue
and of cocks' slaughtered throats cut to no avail
for the well-being of a turban
which for a long time now has been
no more than a heap of dust
smirking under a slab
while in the shade of a fig tree
women and candles burn
to do magic with the eye
bad luck
and the raven of despair.

For an amulet did I too
swap my gold tooth
and the henna on my hands
and unclasp my eyes,
did I too look at the moon
and drink bowls
of the liquid verb, still and black?
I also kept staring
at the boats and the storks which were leaving
but we women all waited
                    in vain
in tears
for our fathers, loved ones
sons and brothers.

But the city opens wide the jaws
of its prisons
swallows them with its tea
and then fans itself.
But the city pulls its knives
whittles us a body without limbs
a face without a voice
but the city bears its heart
as we do our walls,
but the city . . .
I hurt even down to my shadow cast
upon the other sidewalk
where my latest poems are strewn
in little crystals of opaque salts
like icy tears.
My head falls down on my chest
like a mortar shell
seen from close up, my heart is a lake.

Translated by Eric Sellin

[I think of the land and the wheat]

I think of the land and the wheat
richer after the battle,
of this flower of irreplaceable blood.
Man with a prisoner's profile
contemporary of all times,
mute like a tree of winter,
listen.
Under the tent wind carries the birds,
the child sleeps dreaming of a red sea
and the dew on eyelids.
What more does war need?
A road, someone living, someone dead,
a river of sacred mud,
and the devouring heat of June.
A clock, a wall, an old sabre,
a head forgotten at the top of the stairway,
a bedouin white against the background of sand,
and the double noise of fear.

Translated by Elaine Gardiner

Maybe Then

Maybe if you saw Hiroshima
I mean Hiroshima mon amour
if you saw
if you spent two hours suffering like a dog
if you saw
how much it can hurt hurt burn
and twist the soul like that iron
strip away joy forever
like charred skin
and you saw that nevertheless
there are ways to go on to live stay around
bearing no visible wounds
I mean
then
maybe then you'd believe
maybe then you'd suffer
understand.

Translated by Louise Popkin

PART FOUR

"Now That I'm Helpless"

MOTHERS IN AMBIGUITY

The Envelope

It is true, Martin Heidegger, as you have written,
I *fear to cease*, even knowing that at the hour
of my death my daughters will absorb me, even
knowing they will carry me about forever
inside them, an arrested fetus, even as I carry
the ghost of my mother under my navel, a nervy
little androgynous person, a miracle
folded in lotus position.

Like those old pear-shaped Russian dolls that open
at the middle to reveal another and another, down

to the pea-sized, irreducible minim,
may we carry our mothers forth in our bellies.
May we, borne onward by our daughters, ride
in the Envelope of Almost-Infinity,
that chain letter good for the next twenty-five
thousand days of their lives.

from Christmas in Africa

One autumn afternoon when I was nine
feeding the chickens near the grapevine, brooding
in sunshine, my mother asked me to choose

a christmas present that year.
Anything I said, but a doll. Whatever you choose
but not a doll

my faith in her to know
better than I could myself what gift would please me.
And so at the height of summer

we made our pilgrimage
to the earth's greenest riches and the ample ocean.
And christmas eve

was three white daughters
three bright angels singing silent night as my mother
lit the candles

the tree blooming
sea breathing, the beloved son in his cradle sleeping.
Over the hills and skies

on his sleigh the father
the awaited one, made his visitation. Weeks of dreaming
and wondering now

in a box in my hand.
Shoebox size. Not waterwings then or a time machine no
something the size

of a pair of shoes.
Not a pony then or a river canoe. Not a new dress no.
I pulled at the bright bowed ribbons

and little christmas angels
with trembling hands. Underneath the monkey-apple branch
dressed up in baubles and tinsel

and blobs of cotton wool
the sea soaring, stars and the fairy at the treetop
shining

his hand on my shoulder
my mother's eyes on my face two burning suns
piercing my mind and in the box

a doll.
A stupid pretty empty thing. Pink smiling girl. The world
rocked about my head

my face fell into a net
from that moment. My heart in me played possum
and never recovered.

I said I liked the wretched thing
joy broke over my face like a mirror cracking. I said it
so loud, so often

I almost believed it. All that christmas
a shameful secret bound me and the doll and my mother
irrevocably together.

When I knew she was watching
I would grab for the doll in the night, or take it
tenderly with me to the beach

wrapped in a small towel.
At last on the last night of the journey home
staying at a hotel

my mother woke me early
to go out and find the maid. In my pyjamas, half asleep
I staggered out into the dawn

heat rising like mist
from the ground, birds making an uproar, snakes
not yet awake

a sense of something
about to happen under the heavy damp rustle
of the trees.

My feet left footprints
in the dew. When I returned I was clutching that precious
corpse to my chest

like one of the bereaved.
Now I know, said my mother, that although you didn't
want a doll, you really do love her.

I was believed!
Something fell from my face with a clatter—
my punishment was over

and in that moment
fell from my mother's face a particular smile, a kind of
dear and tender curling of the eyes

fell. Two gripped faces
side by side on the floor, smiled at each other
before we grabbed them back

and fitted them with a hollow rattle
to our love. And I laid the doll down in a suitcase
and slammed the lid on its face

and never looked at it again.
And in a sense my mother did the same, and in a sense
my punishment and hers

had always been, and just begun.

Brown Circle

My mother wants to know
why, if I hate
family so much,
I went ahead and

had one. I don't
answer my mother.
What I hated
was being a child,
having no choice about
what people I loved.

I don't love my son
the way I meant to love him.
I thought I'd be
the lover of orchids who finds
red trillium growing
in the pine shade, and doesn't
touch it, doesn't need
to possess it. What I am
is the scientist,
who comes to that flower
with a magnifying glass
and doesn't leave, though
the sun burns a brown
circle of grass around
the flower. Which is
more or less the way
my mother loved me.

I must learn
to forgive my mother,
now that I'm helpless
to spare my son.

To My Little Girl

She was little,
She did not know the use of shoes;
I warned her of the brambles in the bush, in the briars,
She laughed trampling my words,
Briars, under naked feet;
She knows, I sighed
There are no shoes which she can wear for briars,
brambles,
For she has seen me bleed,
Seen me bruised,
With my feet clothed and covered.

The Mirror of Matsuyama

Daughter, this I give you before I die.
When you are lonely, take out this mirror.
I will be with you always.
  —from a Japanese folktale

Mother, what trick of light
brings you back—your face rising to the surface?
Is it my need that imprisons you behind
the cold glass? When you lay still,
the flowered quilt no longer warm with your body,
I didn't believe your promise.
                    Days passed,
and even the pauses between my breath
would remind me that you are not here.
But remembering your words, I held
your mirror before me.
                    Amazed,
you looked back, your fingers stretched
to meet mine. Between us, I could feel
only the glass. The brown centers of your eyes
returned my stare.
                    Mother, how do you see me?
Enclosed within your reflection, you can't answer
what I ask—how your teacup knows
the shape of my hands, the smooth rim
the bow of my lips. With every stroke
of my brush, why do I imagine the length
of your hair?
                    Each time we meet, we press
closer together, as if you could make me whole.

To My Daughter

Daughter, lying on a snow-white bed
far away in a hospital,
are you weaving midnight into day
with the dark threads of pain?

Don't be depressed.
When we, too full of life,
rush about too much and need rest,
the Goddess of Creation offers us a sickbed.
Lie back, be refreshed; reinvigorate yourself.
There are so many steps still to be climbed.

Reading your poems in this dew-wet courtyard
I wonder whether the spirit in you,
which makes life blossom,
hurt you more than the body
that grew inside me like a flower.
These cocoons you've spun,
to put to sleep the worms
gnawing at your core,
burst open; and wings,
jostling, fluttering, rising,
swarm my mind.

Your mind may grow restless with unhappy thoughts,
your body may be weary of household tasks,
but I have no fears for you.
Your power to turn worms into butterflies
comforts me.

The Gift

Lord, You may not recognize me
speaking for someone else.
I have a son. He is
so little, so ignorant.

He likes to stand
at the screen door, calling
oggie, *oggie*, entering
language, and sometimes
a dog will stop and come up
the walk, perhaps
accidentally. May he believe
this is not an accident?
At the screen
welcoming each beast
in love's name, Your emissary.

Dreams in Harrison Railroad Park

We sit on a green bench in Harrison Railroad Park.
As we rest, I notice my mother's thighs
thin as my wrists.
I want to hug her
but I am afraid.

A bearded man comes by, asks for a cigarette.
We shake our heads, hold out our empty hands.
He shuffles away and picks up
a half-smoked stub.
His eyes light up.
Enclosed by the sun he dreams
temporarily.

Across the street an old woman hobbles by.
My mother tells me: She is unhappy here.
She thinks she would be happier
back home.
But she has forgotten.

My mother's neighbor dreams
of warm nights in Shanghai,
of goldfish swimming in a courtyard pond,
of having a young maid
anoint her tiny bound feet.

And my mother dreams
of wearing dresses that hang in her closet,
of swallowing soup without pain,
of coloring eggs
for an unborn grandson.

I turn and touch my mother's eyes.
They are wet
and I dream
and I dream
of embroidering
new skin.

I Have Gone into My Prison Cell

I have gone into my prison cell
You are my guard,
And freedom my chain
I know that you guard me well
Against myself;
I may just ask too much
Or think too little
To fit your pattern
Or I may just want to breathe
The cool night air
And watch if the stars are really blue at night;
And of course you know that
Nights are sombre things
Not for contemplation or for light
And it's better to discuss things abstruse by day
When the night's enchantment
Will not make me feel my chains
Or hear the clanging of doors.

YUKO KAWANO

[Climbing the mountain pass]

Climbing the mountain pass
our two children
between us:
this is
a family.

Translated by Leza Lowitz, Miyuki Aoyama, and Akemi Tomioka

Paper Boat—Sent to Mother

I never throw away a piece a paper.
   I always save it.
I fold it into a tiny boat
   And cast it into the sea.

Some boats blow into a porthole;
   Some get drenched by the waves and stick to the bow.
I still fold paper boats every day,
   Hoping that one will float where I wish it to.

Mother, if you see a little white boat in your dream,
   Do not think, startled, that it comes for no reason.
It was folded by your dearest daughter, with teary eyes,
   Who begged it to sail across the miles with her smile
      and her sorrow.

Translated by Michelle Yeh

Springwater, Part 105

Creator,
   If in eternal life
   Only one wish is granted,
I will plead in all sincerity:
   "Let me be in my mother's arms,
   Let Mother be in a small boat,
   Let the small boat be on a moonlit sea."

Translated by Michelle Yeh

Rocking

The sea rocks her thousands of waves.
The sea is divine.
Hearing the loving sea
I rock my son.

The wind wandering by night
rocks the wheat.
Hearing the loving wind
I rock my son.

God, the Father, soundlessly rocks
His thousands of worlds.
Feeling His hand in the shadow
I rock my son.

Translated by Doris Dana

PART FIVE

"Who Stopped the Dance?"

DOMESTIC BATTLEFIELDS

In the Fist of Your Hatred

Like a worm I writhe in your tight fist
As you try to smother my voice
And my mind with your brutal grip;
Fear stalks the house of my brain
As your pepper-red eyes shout blood.

Your grip strangles my tongue
Your fingers sprinkle seeds of fear in my mind
And it sprouts like a raging bush fire.
You have set up fear as my companion
And I cringe from your bloodshot eyes.

Secret alarm bells sear my brain
And leave me burning with a wild rage
For I will not let fear swallow
My breath, my dreams, and my hopes!
My hidden courage will saw off your fist.

Girl in the Kitchen

Like other things
they say a kitchen too
means many things
but for this girl
this kitchen is her house
this that and every house
even the house of burial

Just as every creature
has a stomach
every house has a kitchen
I don't know whose plan it is
no windows no doors
not even a chimney for the smoke
not even a hole somewhere—
she longs for one

As she cooks—
the birds outside
the noise of playing children
buses cars autorickshaws running
into the distance
even to the seashore
but she ignores them
as she grinds the spices
renunciation comes easy
doesn't it
when you have nothing?

Yet sometimes if she hears
the airplane in the sky
the plane! the plane! she cries
from where she is
what trips can she take
while she's with salt and tamarind?

the twenty-first century?
will you take me with you?
the sound in the sky
melts away
v e r y   s l o w l y

This B.C. girl in the kitchen
blows *foo foo* into the fire
and sings
surely there's someone
up there in the plane
a gentleman in make-up and costume
as surely as all creatures are born
to steal and to cry

Maybe the flying chariot
will flap its wings
break through the roof
let down a ladder
lift me up as I peel potatoes
and make me the chief queen

O Rama Rama! carrying me
to Lanka or to Ayodhya?
old names and places
heard many times before
now what about worlds
no one has heard of?
fly to those worlds
I command you

And so on —
she weaves songs this girl
her ears open to the sounds in the sky
breaking the stalks of green peppers
her lifetime getting spent
drop by drop

Translated by A. K. Ramanujan

The Conservation of Energy

Why was that door locked? I want
the front door open when I get home,

and the lights on, the minute
you hear me honking. He slams

the door behind him, dashes
the porcelain bowl from the table.

Drips of oil shiver to the floor,
fork and knife, little wings

of frayed lettuce. A few
bleak words bitten off and I snap

at our son, who enters
laughing. And now

the child is pulling the cat's tail
with both hands. The cat

is storing up minus signs like a battery,
sharpening its claws.

The Felling of a Tree

When the air is a sharpened blade,
cutting nostrils clean like cutlass steel,
the bush-planters pass the sleeping houses.
Sometimes alone, sometimes in pairs,
they lumber up the mountain road tall-
tops pounding the asphalt smooth.

Sometimes I awake and follow them,
knowing they go beyond the road's end
into the depths of bearded trees,
where tallness is not neighbours' fences
and bigness is not the swollen houses
that swallow us all.

I follow—slowly—my thinking measured;
my steps behind clobbering boots, steady,
knowing that if I stay in neat clearings
I will never see, and I want to see the trees,
I want to hear their long silences speaking,
leaves whispering secrets in my starved ears.

I follow, drinking the air like water,
my steps a soft conversation with blades
that cut paths for themselves through asphalt.
I follow, the strength in my thighs a newness
that makes my feet sprout roots,
and I think: This is what tall means.

Just when my lips begin to savour my salt,
he looks back, and seeing me growing branches
draws out his cutting steel and slashes my feet,
since girls can never become trees.

Turning, I run down the mountain weeping,
weeping like leaves after lashings
from rain-forest showers.

Tears

There is a scream that binds my heart to
    the throat of the Earth
And that foam is
my lost voice.

My robe illusion
My necklace of counterfeit stone
All that is the world may be
deceit
but my tears.

I am the woman bleeding the sharpened years
I come and go behind
Tall windows.
a woman in veils about to flee
My childhood smashed by this
nightmare.

Translated by Kamal Boullata

My Pain

To Zhaozhao, my forever remembered sister

your childhood
and mine
walked away hand in hand
in a fast falling dusk
you and I stood at the forked road
separated
by distance

sadness paved the returning path
I couldn't gather all the broken memories

the Fusong flower was still impetuous then
it lit a small crimson lantern
but failed to brighten the day
the accumulated sorrow streamed down
urged me to look for
your naughty eyes—
 expecting life
 and a future

finally I awoke in a dying flash of light
abandoned the forgotten attempt
 I'd rather suffer the pain of the heavy burden
 than consent to light emptiness

Translated by Tang Chao with Lee Robinson

The Well

To the right
of our hill
there's a shining well
full of water.
Last year
summer covered it
with green mango blossom.
The green tempted
a calf,
which fell in
and drowned.
Since then
people have stopped
drinking from that well.
Now, like a thief,
I bathe in it
at night.
I cup my hands
and drink from it
at night.
But the water
doesn't quench
my thirst, my desire.
In the dark depths
of the well
there are shadows
still waiting for
the girls
who'd slung a rope
on its hook
but never came back
to draw water.
The well's darkness
is waiting
for the moment

when I'll have
the courage
to stretch out my hands
and drink its water
in broad daylight.

Translated by Iqbal Masud

Rain

A teacher asked Paul
what he would remember
from third grade, and he sat
a long time before writing
"this year sumbody tutched me
on the sholder"
and turned his paper in.
Later she showed it to me
as an example of her wasted life.
The words he wrote were large
as houses in a landscape.
He wanted to go inside them
and live, he could fill in
the windows of "o" and "d"
and be safe while outside
birds building nests in drainpipes
knew nothing of the coming rain.

Who Stops the Dance?

Like wild tea blossoms
One white skirt
Follows another white skirt.
Parasols open like a thousand petals—
Corpses of dreams—
A thousand petals of the falling Spring.
I want to pull you to pieces—
My heart full of weary anxiety.
Who spilled life over this meadow?
Who stopped the dance?
Who smashed the dream?
Who trampled the Spring?
Fate.
Tomorrow you must obey.
Yes, I want to pull you to pieces—
White skirt, white skirt
As weariness and anxiety
Overwhelm my heart.

Translated by Kenneth Rexroth and Ling Chung

Say You Love Me

What happened earlier I'm not sure of.
Of course he was drunk, but often he was.
His face looked like a ham on a hook above

me—I was pinned to the chair because
he'd hunkered over me with arms like jaws
pried open by the chair arms. "Do you love

me?" he began to sob. "Say you love me!"
I held out. I was probably fifteen.
What had happened? Had my mother—had she

said or done something? Or had he just been
drinking too long after work? "He'll get *mean*,"
my sister hissed, "just *tell* him." I brought my knee

up to kick him, but was too scared. Nothing
could have got the words out of me then. Rage
shut me up, yet "DO YOU?" was beginning

to peel, as of live layers of skin, age
from age from age from him until he gazed
through hysteria as a wet baby thing

repeating, "Do you love me? Say you do,"
in baby chokes, only loud, for they came
from a man. There wouldn't be a rescue

from my mother, still at work. The same
choking sobs said, "Love me, love me," and my game
was breaking down because I couldn't do

anything, not escape into my own
refusal, *I won't, I won't*, not fantasize
a kind, rich father, not fill the narrowed zone,

empty except for confusion until the size
of my fear ballooned as I saw his eyes,
blurred taurean—my sister screamed—unknown,

unknown to me, a voice rose and leveled
off, "I love you," I said. *"Say 'I love you,
Dad!'"* "I love you, Dad," I whispered, leveled

by defeat into a cardboard image, untrue,
unbending. I was surprised I could move
as I did to get up, but he stayed, burled

onto the chair—my monstrous fear—she screamed,
my sister, "Dad, the phone! Go answer it!"
The phone wasn't ringing, yet he seemed

to move toward it, and I ran. He had a fit—
"It's not ringing!"—but I was at the edge of it
as he collapsed into the chair and blamed

both of us at a distance. No, the phone
was not ringing. There was no world out there,
so there we remained, completely alone.

On the Turning Up of Unidentified Black Female Corpses

Mowing his three acres with a tractor,
a man notices something ahead—a mannequin—
he thinks someone threw it from a car. Closer
he sees it is the body of a black woman.

The medics come and turn her with pitchforks.
Her gaze shoots past him to nothing. Nothing
is explained. How many black women
have been turned up to stare at us blankly,

in weedy fields, off highways,
pushed out in plastic bags,
shot, knifed, unclothed partially, raped,
their wounds sealed with a powdery crust.

Last week on TV, a gruesome face, eyes bloated shut.
No one will say, "She looks like she's sleeping," ropes
of blue-black slashes at the mouth. Does anybody
know this woman? Will any come forth? Silence

like a backwave rushes into that field
where, just the week before, four other black girls
had been found. The gritty image hangs in the air
just a few seconds, but it strikes me,

a black woman, there is a question being asked
about my life. How can I
protect myself? Even if I lock my doors,
walk only in the light, someone wants me dead.

Am I wrong to think
if five white women had been stripped,
broken, the sirens would wait until
someone was named?

Is it any wonder I walk over these bodies
pretending they are not mine, that I do not know
the killer, that I am just like any woman—
if not wanted, at least tolerated.

Part of me wants to disappear, to pull
the earth on top of me. Then there is this part
that digs me up with this pen
and turns my sad black face to the light.

Infanticide

Sometimes they were put in baskets, little nests
of rushes and leaves. (Someone had to weave
these water-cradles for them—the threading
fingers of grandmother, auntie, midwife.)
They were placed in their casket-boats
and launched, and if they couldn't swim,
whose fault was that?

Some were curled, heads touching knees,
in their womb positions inside clay jars,
then set along temple porticoes
in case some passing worshipper might want
a baby for a slave. Their fretting
voices in the corridors were as common
and hoarse as dry cicadas, till they died.

Some were burned for expiation to the gods,
in ceremonies, shrill trumpets and cymbals
covering their cries. Some were placed naked,
still bloody, on icy pinnacles in dark snow.
Some were strangled, some tortured
to death, some eaten, a few hours old.
After all, nobody knew them yet.

Some were flung off canyon cliffs,
even on a spring afternoon, the prairie
colored with clover and milkvetch,
or even on a damp autumn morning,
the plums red and sweet and fragrant.

Mary Hamilton bore her baby alone
in the King's forest, leaning back, pressing
against an oak, her skirts pulled up,
and all the while watching the patterns
above her, layered leaves, sky pieces,

branches and boughs constricting, widening
with the wind. Then she killed it with a knife.

Gone, murdered by deliberate
acts—I don't think anyone
ever counted them all—those cursed, born
during lightning storms or under a bad
moon or feetfirst or blind, born
during war or a hard journey, into starvation,
those with the wrong fathers, the girls,
the unwanted. It was the custom,
and there were reasons, burdens.
Even mothers said so.

From every stone-cut or gnawed
umbilical, from every bud-sized
fist, every thumb and finger petal
folded inward, from every perfectly
stitched violet thread, every temple pulse,
every rib shudder of this elegy,
relieve us.

Will You Marry Me?

I never go anywhere—
I've cut down all the trees in my backyard
and pulled up all the grass around me.
People bore children
and the children went to war
when they came back
the children bore children—
there are children everywhere.
But the women, they simply bathe.
It will all be over soon
perhaps the grass will grow
and people will die in the grass.

Translated by Leza Lowitz and Miyuki Aoyama

Dearest Love—I

Dearest love, listen:
after the cave where death's artillery blazed in the mind,
where bullets are fields, houses, chimneys
the dead heaped like frozen waves,
when at flood tide the Bedouin wind raged through the
    camps,
their deadly steeds galloping to triumph
after terror,
after my heart was torn out,
after the knock-out,
we woke up to live again.

Forgive one who came back from the dead,
who saw what he saw,
who saved himself in time.
From the black cloud I saved myself
but when new life came my way,
I walked proudly
in the dusty graveyards of our dead.
But ah, love of my life,
you weren't there, and so
I married my cousin after all.

Translated by Charles Doria

Tattoo Writing

Not with your tribe's spears I write
   for they are dull
   but with my nails
Words without walls.
Sister,
For you I have inscribed
   Love-songs
   weaving the sun's rays
   to your latticed window.

To tell me you accept
   The Tribe's traditions and prescriptions
   is a concession
   to being buried alive.
The noble inch or two
    of tattoo
   over your skin
Shall carve a bottomless night
   into
your flesh.

It pains me
to see The Tribe dwell
in you sprawling
in your college seat not unlike
   your grandmother
   who thought she was
   a lottery ticket won
   at home. A woman
in her twenties
sitting before some tent
shrouded with robes and veils
carrying the spindle
but does not spin.
To hear you talk

about a cloak
the clan's men bought
for you;
to hear your boast
about blue-blood
the heirs
and chip off the old oak tree.
The Sheikh's voice in your voice
cancels
you.

Sister
My kingdom does not claim
    dowries of cows and cattle
thus The Tribe rejects me
for you are their legitimate child
I am the one disavowed
You belong to lords of virgin
    lands
I to seasons bleeding flames.

Should The Tribe's drums and barking dogs
Shut off your hearing
        the rippling
    of women's
blood

It doesn't mean
you are without a wound
as being captive of your tent
    doesn't remove
    the sky above.
You may cross deserts
        on camel back
It won't hinder a satellite from
    reaching the moon.
Sister
If you wish to reject me now
Say "no" with your own nails

I only tried
to comb
nocturnal grief
out of your crownless hair.

Translated by Kamal Boullata

Young Wife's Lament

The mule that lived on the road
where I was married
would bray to wake the morning,
but could not wake me.
How many summers I slept
lost in my hair. How many
mules on how many hills singing.
Back of a deep ravine
he lived, above a small river
on a beaten patch of land.
I walked up in the day and walked down,
having been given nothing
else to do. The road grew no longer,
I grew no wiser, my husband
was away selling things to people who buy.
He went up the road, too, but
the road was full of doors for him,
the road was his belt and,
one notch at a time, he loosened it
on his way. I would sit
on the hill of stones and look down
on the trees, on the lake
far away with its boats and those
who ride in boats
and I could not pray. Some of us
have mule minds,
are foolish as sails whipping
in the wind, senseless
as sheets rolling through the fields,
some of us are not given
even a wheel of a tinker's cart
upon which to pray.
When I came back I pumped water
in the yard under the trees
by the fence where the cows came up,

but water is not wisdom
and change is not made by wishes.
Else I would have ridden something,
even a mule, over
those hills and away.

The Grand Get Together

Dedicated to the Karemba Heifer, *his first love-poem to me*

Last night,
We had a Big Get-Together Party
Where men sat by men
And women formed feminine tribes
Or old friends maintained tight circles
Chorusing the same old jokes and ideas
Stunningly unbored.

It was a Get-Together Party
Husbands hedging-in wives
Giving them freedom to dance unfreely.
When spinsters came for their husbands
The wives strove to coat their suspecting fears
And answered throat-constricted

"'s all right—you can take him . . ."
From the start to end
Their eyes were unblinking
To see, to confirm,
The stale life-sucking rumour
Of the Boss-secretary affair.

Then the formal goodbyes
The Thank you very much for the evening ceremonies
And people staggered home—
Singing . . . thinking . . . quarrelling or planning

But the majority fearing
Blankets of fuss and webs of hen-pecking partners
And arrows of indifferent eyes
That were the embraces and kisses of Home.

I too went home,
The children sound asleep
The bedroom twice as large
Darkness and emptiness embraced me
In the room where you and I would form a world.

I pulled out the drawer of your letters
And under the dim light of the bedroom
Read not once nor twice
Your first love-poem to me
The bedding growing lukewarm,
Quite warm . . . and warm . . .
Each time I gluttonously reanalysed
Your first love-poem to me.

Then the ventilators let in vents of ululations
My right-hand neighbours were fighting
They, who together hosted the Get-Together Party
Hardly two hours ago—in the name of Trinary Triumph.

I gripped your love-poem tightly
The one you wrote after six years of togetherness
How more peaceful, more gratifying
To attend this poem of the heart
Than a Big Get-Together Party—
For Ceremony!

My Rival's House

is peopled with many surfaces.
Ormolu and gilt, slipper satin,
lush velvet couches,
cushions so stiff you can't sink in.
Tables polished clear enough to see distortions in.

We take our shoes off at her door,
shuffle stocking-soled, tiptoe—the parquet floor
is beautiful and its surface must
be protected. Dust
cover, drawn shade,
won't let the surface colour fade.

Silver sugar-tongs and silver salver
my rival serves us tea.
She glosses over him and me.
I am all edges, a surface, a shell
and yet my rival thinks she means me well.
But what squirms beneath her surface I can tell.
Soon, my rival
capped tooth, polished nail
will fight, fight foul for her survival.
Deferential, daughterly, I sip
and thank her nicely for each bitter cup.

And I have much to thank her for.
This son she bore—
first blood to her—
never, never can escape scot free
the sour potluck of family.
And oh how close
this family that furnishes my rival's place.

Lady of the house.
Queen bee.

She is far more unconscious,
far more dangerous than me.
Listen, I was always my own worst enemy.
She has taken even this from me.

She dishes up her dreams for breakfast.
Dinner, and her salt tears pepper our soup.
She won't
give up.

If You Think with Fire

If you think with fire
Then life is a road that leads
To waiting for nothing.
On its two sides stand wonderful buildings,
Whose compound eyes brim and flow
With happy songs of great mansions,
And the melancholy of little round houses.

Then there sinks to the bottom
Of a trembling white jade cup
The broken necklace of the past,
Two pieces dazzling the eyes
With their red lustre −
July and March.

If the castle where my dreams are stored
Began to burn,
I would stand bewildered in the rain,
Watching one man,
And so wildly,
Thinking of another.

Translated by Kenneth Rexroth and Ling Chung

The Village

Kanyariri, Village of Toil,
Village of unending work.
Like a never dying spring,
Old women dark and bent
Trudge along with their hoes
To plots of weedy maize.
Young wives with donkeys
From cockcrow to setting of the sun
Go about their timeless duties,
Their scraggy figures like bows set in a row,
Plod up and down the rolling village farms
With loads on their backs
And babies tied to their bellies.
In the fields all day they toil
Stirring up the soil with hands and knives
Like chickens looking for worms.
Nothing here seems to sit still.
Even the village church is like a favourite well
Where the "Revivalists" with their loudspeakers
Never cease calling people
To confess their sins and drink the Water of Life.
At dawn men ride away leaving the womenfolk
To fend for the bony goats and the crying children.

Destruction

I do not know what has destroyed you,
Maybe it was too much of loving
Or too little
Both strangely have the same face—mine
When I look upon my hands
That have caressed you,
Untied corded muscles of pain
On cool sheets
Spreading my hair upon your limbs
To inflame them,
How would I know
That I could darken your eyes
And bring down the blinds
Upon your soul,
Hurt you by wordless thought
Scoop out warmth from your centre,
Leave dark regions of despair—
I do not know how I've destroyed you
Maybe it was too much of loving
Or too little.

A Visit

In a home for incurables
I visited a woman who was about to die.
She embraced me,
I felt through her gray shirt
the tiny bones of her brittle body
which would no longer arouse lust or tenderness.

"I don't want this, take me away."
Near us, a retarded woman was vomiting.

Translated by Czesław Miłosz and Leonard Nathan

Woman

She, the river,
said to him, the sea:
    All my life
    I've been dissolving myself
    and flowing towards you
    for your sake
    in the end it was I
    who turned into the sea
    a woman's gift
    is as large as the sky
        but you went on
        worshipping yourself
        you never thought
        of becoming a river
        and merging
        with me

Translated by Vinay Dharwadker

Two Women Knitting

Rama says,
Rama says to Uma,
Oh my,
How time passes.
Ah me, says Uma.
Then both fall silent.

The two women go on casting stitches.
They skip stitches, slip the skipped stitches over,
Knit over purl,
Purl over knit.
After many intricate loops and cables,
Their dark secrets still lie locked inside them,
They've thrown the keys to their jewellery boxes into the
        lake.
Insert the keys, and the locks will bleed real blood.

Two women knit,
Clicking metal on metal,
Passers-by look up amazed at the sparks that fly.
Loneliness turns up at every other row
Of stitches in their patterns,
Even though they've worn each other's saris
And bathed each other's slippery infants,
Even though at this very moment
Their husbands lie asleep in the rooms upstairs,
Shaking them in their dreams.

Translated by the poet and Arlene Zide

The Gypsy

A late afternoon in July, too early to begin
making supper, too hot
to work in the garden.
A Saturday, then, and after

the war, for the three of them
are there: mother, father, daughter.
But what should be clear,
should be said, from the start
is that the father
always doubts, can't be sure
this is his
daughter and so has pulled
back gradually to the edges
of the house, re-entering
only in fury and shame.

But now he is sleeping.
Her mother and she look in the doorway
at this man, on his back,
completely clothed, against
the candlewick spread.
He is snoring, his mouth
precisely locked into a wide,
slightly vibrating O.
From the doorway they can see
his arms wide, his palms up,
his shoes in opposing directions.

Whose idea was it?
They say they can't remember,
but one of them goes
to the sliding velvet trays
of the jewel box and untangles
a green crystal earring,

then attaches it
with delicate turns of the vise
to his left, slightly tufted,
lobe. The green globe
dangles from its chain
to the pillow, casting a bright
leafy shadow.

Next a vermilion disk for
the right ear, a white plastic bow
for his hair:
the room seems hotter, more still, by now
and the locusts start to wind
into a wilder cadenza.
When he stops snoring

they try to hold their breath,
but his mouth lies slack
in deeper sleep, his breathing
pale and regular.
By this point they have taken
out the cigar-box cache
of brushes, tubes, and puffs.
They powder his coarse cheeks
layer by layer and draw the faintly
bruising blusher down
his jaw: they stencil
the eyebrows to match
the latest style—1946,
a year of constant,
mild surprises.

Brazenly, they flourish
the mascara's viscous wand:
and then the fiery lipstick; what red
lips and coal-black lashes!
They discover, for the first time,
they can't look at each other.

As dusk falls, they sit on the porch
and wait—snapping beans,
shelling peas, for supper. When he finally wakes
he is hungry, sour, and dazed a little from sleep;
he cuts everything with his fork, scrapes
his plate, without a word
goes out for the night.
When he's gone the house
seems to fill with a hundred random sounds—
the dishes jarring, the tick
and hum of someone's mower,
an idling car, the darning needles
hovering, some dogs, and then
a bright disk clack-clacking
on the spokes of a distant bicycle.

The mother says, "He's looking
like a gypsy." They wonder
how long this spell can last—
this invention as new
as a homemade fairy tale
where the father,
who is always the real father,
never bothers to look in the mirror.
And those who have lived in
the giant's shadow
for years, find one day
they can speak, they can speak.

Weathering Out

She liked mornings the best—Thomas gone
to look for work, her coffee flushed with milk,

outside autumn trees blowsy and dripping.
Past the seventh month she couldn't see her feet

so she floated from room to room, houseshoes flapping,
navigating corners in wonder. When she leaned

against a door jamb to yawn, she disappeared entirely.

Last week they had taken a bus at dawn
to the new airdock. The hangar slid open in segments

and the zeppelin nosed forward in its silver envelope.
The men walked it out gingerly, like a poodle,

then tied it to a mast and went back inside.
Beulah felt just that large and placid, a lake;

she glistened from cocoa butter smoothed in
when Thomas returned every evening nearly

in tears. He'd lean an ear on her belly
and say: *Little fellow's really talking,*

though to her it was more the *pok-pok-pok*
of a fingernail tapping a thick cream lampshade.

Sometimes during the night she woke and found him
asleep there and the child sleeping, too.

The coffee was good but too little. Outside
everything shivered in tinfoil—only the clover

between the cobblestones hung stubbornly on,
green as an afterthought. . . .

Morning Exercises

I wake up and say: I'm through.
It's my first thought at dawn.
What a nice way to start the day
with such a murderous thought.

God, take pity on me
—is the second thought, and then
I get out of bed
and live as if
nothing had been said.

Translated by Andrea Deletant and Brenda Walker

Thinking of Someone

For you I have stored up an ocean of thought,
Quiet, transparent, bright.
Your arms encircle the city of sleep
Of my far off, beautiful dreams.

A lamp shines faintly through a crescent window.
It is your name, changed to gold and silver silk,
That has wrapped me and entangled me
With half a century.

An ocean of thoughts
All stored in that quiet city moat—
The most beautiful language,
Sounds like beautiful flower petals,
That fall and clothe my body with dream.

Translated by Kenneth Rexroth and Ling Chung

PART SIX

"It Is the Time of Awakening"

REACHING AND REBUILDING

Flowers No Longer Fly in Our City

Flowers no longer fly in our city in March
Monstrous buildings squat everywhere—
Sphinxes in the desert, squinting at you in mockery
And a pack of urban tigers howl
From morning to night

From morning to night
The downpour of pitch-black smoke, the thunder of the
    city
Squabbles between cogwheels
Conflicts between machines
Time broken into pieces, life fading away by the moment

At night our city is like a poisonous spider
Extending its web
To snare pedestrians

The loneliness of the heart
The emptiness of the night

I often sit quietly in the dreamless field
To watch the city at the bottom of the night, like
An incomparably large diamond brooch
On display in the window of an import boutique
Waiting for someone to pay an exorbitant price.

Translated by Michelle Yeh

Lunch in Nablus City Park

When you lunch in a town which has recently known war
under a calm slate sky mirroring none of it,
certain words feel impossible in the mouth.
Casualty: too casual, it must be changed.
A short man stacks mounds of pita bread
on each end of the table, muttering
something about more to come.
Plump birds landing on park benches
surely had their eyes closed recently,
must have seen nothing of weapons or blockades.
When the woman across from you whispers
I don't think we can take it anymore
and you say there are people praying for her
in the mountains of Himalaya and she says
Lady, it is not enough, then what?

A plate of cigar-shaped meatballs, dish of tomato,
friends dipping bread—
I will not marry till there is true love, says one,
throwing back her cascade of perfumed hair.
He says the University of Texas seems remote to him
as Mars, and last month he stayed in his house
for 26 days. He will not leave, he refuses to leave.
In the market they are selling
men's shoes with air-vents, a beggar displays
the giant scab of leg he must drag from alley to alley,
and students gather to discuss what constitutes
genuine protest.

In summers, this cafe is full.
Today only our table sends laughter into the trees.
What cannot be answered checkers the tablecloth
between the squares of white and red.
Where do the souls of hills hide

when there is shooting in the valleys?
What makes a man with a gun seem bigger
than a man with almonds? How can there be war
and the next day eating, a man stacking plates
on the curl of his arm, a table of people
toasting one another in languages of grace:
For you who came so far;
For you who held out, wearing a black scarf
to signify grief;
For you who believe true love can find you
amidst this atlas of tears linking one town
to its own memory of mortar,
when it was still a dream to be built
and people moved here, believing,
and someone with sky and birds in his heart
said this would be a good place for a park.

Meditation on the Threshold

No, throwing yourself under a train like Tolstoy's Anna
is not the answer,
nor hastening Madame Bovary's arsenic
nor waiting for the angel with the javelin
to reach the parapets of Avila
before you tie the kerchief to your head
and begin to act.

Nor intuiting the laws of geometry,
counting the beams in your cell
like Sor Juana. The answer is not
to write while visitors arrive
in the Austen living room
nor to lock yourself in the attic
of some New England house
and dream, the Dickinson family Bible
beneath your spinster's pillow.

There must be some other way whose name is not Sappho
or Mesaline or Mary of Egypt
or Magdalene or Clemencia Isaura . . .

Another way of being free and human.

Another way of being.

Translated by Magda Bogin

He Is Gone

The finger of death touched me,
the world tumbled down
on me.

I am lying under the rubble,
hands broken,
legs broken,
backbone mangled.

People are passing
at a distance.
I call. They do not hear,
They have passed. I am dying.

The dearest man arrives.
He looks for a moment. Does not understand anything.
Leaves.

He is tenderhearted,
he is gone to comfort others.

Translated by Czesław Miłosz and Leonard Nathan

He Was Lucky

To Prof. Władysław Tatarkiewicz

The old man
leaves his house, carries books.
A German soldier snatches the books
flings them in the mud.

The old man picks them up,
the soldier hits him in the face.

The old man falls,
the soldier kicks him and walks away.

The old man
lies in mud and blood.
Under him he feels
the books.

Translated by Magnus J. Krynski and Robert A. Maguire

Returning from the Enemy, Part 6

When the enemy went after my father he spared no weapon
because he wanted, he said, my father's soul.

But it was the land he was after—this beautiful land of
harbor and sweet grass, of palm tree and oak, of black
earth, of red—

And we know that this earth cannot be owned by dictator
or church, by corporation or maker or signer of paper.

He took the land and moved all his relatives in. And when
other immigrants arrived from other lands he denied them
what he had wanted for himself.

Though he wanted them for his customers.

The enemy made a circle of piss to claim us.

He cut everything down to make his cities and factories
    and burned

the forest to plant his fields. The wound so deep

it can be seen far above this blue green planet, far above us.

You cannot destroy a soul though you may destroy a planet.

You cannot destroy a song though you can make a people
    forgetful.

A soul can appear to be destroyed, and a song can
disappear for a few generations only to reemerge from
the heart of a child who turns and becomes a woman.

Puddle

blood and tears of the Ice Age
can even be found in the calyx of a rose.
I can't help feeling that
we're all just slowly vanishing
here in this diluvial age
when we're sleeping
with mammoths.

I can't help feeling that
the people I love are just piling up
in the ridges of the earth
holding up the sky
in no particular rush
to die
relaxed,
just reading,
and singing.

Translated by Leza Lowitz and Miyuki Aoyama

Who Remains Standing?

First,
erase your name,
unravel your years,
destroy your surroundings,
uproot what you seem,
and who remains standing?
Then,
rewrite your name,
restore your age,
rebuild your house,
pursue your path,
and then,
endlessly,
start over, all over again.

Translated by Samuel Hazo and Mirène Ghossein

"I Will Live and Survive"

I will live and survive and be asked:
How they slammed my head against a trestle,
How I had to freeze at nights,
How my hair started to turn grey . . .
But I'll smile. And will crack some joke
And brush away the encroaching shadow.
And I will render homage to the dry September
That became my second birth.
And I'll be asked: "Doesn't it hurt you to remember?"
Not being deceived by my outward flippancy.
But the former names will detonate my memory—
Magnificent as old cannon.
And I will tell of the best people in all the earth,
The most tender, but also the most invincible,
How they said farewell, how they went to be tortured,
How they waited for letters from their loved ones.
And I'll be asked: what helped us to live
When there were neither letters nor any news—only walls,
And the cold of the cell, and the blather of official lies,
And the sickening promises made in exchange for betrayal.
And I will tell of the first beauty
I saw in captivity.
A frost-covered window! No spyholes, nor walls,
Nor cell-bars, nor the long-endured pain—
Only a blue radiance on a tiny pane of glass,
A cast pattern—none more beautiful could be dreamt!
The more clearly you looked, the more powerfully
    blossomed
Those brigand forests, campfires and birds!
And how many times there was bitter cold weather
And how many windows sparkled after that one—
But never was it repeated,
That upheaval of rainbow ice!

And anyway, what good would it be to me now,
And what would be the pretext for that festival?
Such a gift can only be received once,
And perhaps is only needed once.

Translated by David McDuff

from Shajarit

Life is nothing but time:
Where a few sprigs of bougainvillea in a vase of water
are enough—we have a garden!
Because we die alone. And because death is enough to
    awaken us
from this first dream of living, and as we left the movies my
    grandmother
        said
Dream that it is lovely, muchacha—the dream of life
The candle flame rusts
and I, where am I?
I am what continues forever. The surprise of being
I am back to the place of origin, where beginnings begin
This is the time
It is the time of awakening
The old woman lights her Sabbath candles from her death
    and she watches
        me
The Sabbath expands till never, till after, till before
My grandmother who died of dreams
endlessly stirs the dream that she invented
and I invent. A wild girl watches me from my inmost self

I am intact

Translated by Stephen Tapscott

Photograph from Berlin

Memory is the land standing still
for a moment, then a wave covers it.

Snapshots are shields—
what we remember in some way protects us.

In this particular one you're standing
on the balcony of your mother's house
waving at the soldiers passing through.

One of them, a handsome blond,
has caught your eye as he climbs
onto his friends' shoulders
to offer you something, some bread
or a piece of fruit,

his lieutenant's cap
poised over his heart
in a delicate cartoon of love.

Behind you the sky seems to float in all
directions, but the light holds
everything in place.

You cannot know how your life
will measure up against this moment,
your arm frozen in midair.

Your white handkerchief is like a wish.

The Man with the Saxophone

New York. Five A.M.
The sidewalks empty.
Only the steam
pouring from the manhole covers seems alive,
as I amble from shop window to shop window,
sometimes stopping to stare, sometimes not.
Last week's snow is brittle now
and unrecognizable as the soft, white hair
that bearded the face of the city.
I head farther down Fifth Avenue
toward the thirties,
my mind empty
like the buddhists tell you is possible
if only you don't try.
If only I could
turn myself into a bird
like the shaman I was meant to be,
but I can't,
I'm earthbound
and solitude is my companion,
the only one you can count on.
Don't, don't try to tell me otherwise.
I've had it all and lost it
and I never want it back,
only give me this morning to keep,
the city asleep
and there on the corner of Thirty-fourth and Fifth,
the man with the saxophone,
his fingerless gloves caked with grime,
his face also,
the layers of clothes welded to his skin.
I set down my case,
he steps backward
to let me know I'm welcome,
and we stand a few minutes

in the silence so complete
I think I must be somewhere else, not here,
not in this city, this heartland of pure noise.
Then he puts the sax to his lips again
and I raise mine.
I suck the air up from my diaphragm
and bend over into the cold, golden reed,
waiting for the notes to come,
and when they do,
for that one moment,
I'm the unencumbered bird of my imagination,
rising only to fall back
toward concrete,
each note a black flower,
opening, mercifully opening
into the unforgiving new day.

Bluebonnets

I lay down by the side of the road
in a meadow of bluebonnets, I broke
the unwritten law of Texas. My brother

was visiting, he'd been tired, afraid of
his tiredness as we'd driven toward Bremen,
so we stopped for the blue relatives

of lupine, we left the car on huge feet
we'd inherited from our lost father,
our Polish grandfather. Those flowers

were too beautiful to only look at;
we walked on them, stood in the middle
of them, threw ourselves down,

crushing them in their one opportunity
to thrive and bloom. We lay like angels
forgiven our misdeeds, transported

to azure fields, the only word for
the color eluded me — delft, indigo,
sapphire, some heavenly word you might

speak to a sky. I led my terrestrial brother
there to make him smile and this
is my only record of the event.

We took no pictures, we knew no camera
could fathom that blue. I brushed
the soft spikes, I fingered lightly

the delicate earthly petals, I thought,
This is what my hands do well
isn't it, touch things about to vanish.

blessing the boats

at St. Mary's

may the tide
that is entering even now
the lip of our understanding
carry you out
beyond the face of fear
may you kiss
the wind then turn from it
certain that it will
love your back   may you
open your eyes to water
water waving forever
and may you in your innocence
sail through this to that

PART SEVEN

"Listen for Life"

NATURE SPEAKS

Night Shift at the Fruit Cannery

The thin neon light spills on the hands in the tubs,
the pale halves of the pears that must be dipped in salt
    water to

                                keep from turning brown,
the endless procession of cans that moves past the women
now and at midnight and dawn and on and on
even in sleep, even in dream.
Fingers turn wrinkled, turn pale like the pears,
take on a life of their own as they nestle the slippery fruit
                                spoonfashion in the can,
barely stopping to push the straggling hair back under the
    scarf.
No time to talk, no time to look up,
nothing to look up at.
Time has stopped, there is no yesterday, no tomorrow, no
    moment

                        but now, no place but here,
this slave ship hurtling through eons of empty space.
And at the whistle which rends the rumble and clatter and
    din that

                        taught their ears not to hear,
the women stumble outside like children woken too early for
                                school,
stretching stiff limbs and creaking necks, testing a voice
    rusty from

                                lack of use.
Still dazzle-eyed, they look up and see
stars in their multitudes blazing over their heads.

If There Is a

If there is a God, he has a lot to answer for.
Crocuses, purple cups that bloom through snow.
Cerulean, cornflower, azure, turquoise, ultramarine.
Mist off round haybales along the Sand Road
just after 5 A.M., when the foxes go to ground.
Not only the obvious evils, but also these other things
we should not mistake for easy.

Footpaths Cross in the Rice Field

You are horizontal.
I am vertical.
We divide the heavenly bodies
And the four directions between us.
We come from the place of becoming,
Pass by here,
And encounter each other
In this final meeting
In a flooded rice field.
An egret descends on still wings.
We quietly chat about the weather,
And say, "I'll see you again."
Quietly make an appointment,
Climb two far apart hillsides,
And look back from the summits.
A pure white feather floats down.
As the feather floats down,
Oh, at that moment
We both hope that happiness
May also be like a white bird,
Quietly descending
We hope—
Even though birds
Are creatures with wings.

Translated by Kenneth Rexroth and Ling Chung

Out of Time

My job is to watch leaves fall.
To watch the falling leaves and to read
the autobiography of a beautiful girl who became
rich and sad. And thinking of her
without disdain, to see how the squirrel
replaces the earth once he has stored food.
The moon arced up and shrank
in last night's warm, foggy sky, and I saw her
twinned in a silted lake four hours or so
before dawn. I watched a few degrees of her arc
and came under the trees to listen
to the rest of the night, leaf by leaf. The beautiful girl
was still waiting in 1964 where I'd left her
and another sad thing happened soon.
The moon's blue settled into darkness
and the other blue rose at the top of the trees
and an owl cried out and the lichens and the leaves
became visible. Leaves are not
numberless, just as almost nothing is truly random.
But I am not the angel who enumerates
all rising, all falling, all the births and death
no one sees. To me, the leaves seem
like prime numbers, wholly golden and indivisible
in their infinite series. I cannot say
which one leaf will come down next.
I cannot tell you how the beautiful girl's story
came out, since she is still alive.
Whatever this is, is not what it is to be
a tree or the recording angel, but this moveless,
unpowerful condition is something good.
Even magnificent. I can say that. I can say
there is no end to the soft falling.

Under the Stars

Under the stars
In the space of night
I walked the mountain tops
And knew the wind.
The stillness of the dark
Was mine
And the silence of the snow.
Mine were the frosted wind ferns
On the crouching rocks
And the glitter of their veins.
Mine was the creaking snow,
The mist like rime
And the crinkled gleam of the burns.
Mine too, the blue shadows
The grey, cold glint of ice
And the peace of the moonswept hills.

On a Summer Night

The fireflies floated up from the grass.
At the top of the yard, they signalled
to me. I swiped one from the air
and peeked through the cracks of my fingers
to watch its flicker.

I must spend each night alone with my mirrors
around me: books, photographs, pillows,
and an open space. I do not trust
myself in sleep; I will not drop off
into the leisure of a dream. I am the keeper
of this night and its silences.

We lay in the yard and watched the bats
swoop and scream. I could not believe
their blindness as they dove and punched
at the stars. I held my breathing
so they could not hear me.

Sometimes I sit at this window for hours
with a candle behind me in the room.
No bats pass through this sky. It has
no real darkness. And when I see a star,
I watch it disappear through my fingers.

Winter Night, Glencoe

The hills lie
White on the sky
Moon cold and still.
And I
Spraying frost
From the bound, gagged grass
Listen for life.

But sound is lost
Held
Fastened to ice.
Stars move
In themselves
In the sky
Throwing sparks
To fire smothered snow
Blazing below
While I
Ringing night
From the close barred earth
Search for keys
Listen for life.

A Quartet of Daffodils

I think it must be spring
because yesterday morning on Spadina
there was an Indian woman walking
wrapped in maximum eight yards of sari cloth.
It was sheer and a luminous color
like the nectar of pressed apricots.

A red dot punctuated the center of her brow,
like a small and urgent point of energy
had found its way to the surface of her skin,
and jeweled or a drop of blood, it was gleaming.
I think it must be spring because
there is not a host but a quartet of daffodils

sprung up in the front yard of Gore Vale.
They stand not straight but bowed over so.
I think that they had a hard time making it out
of their frozen birthplace inside the earth.
Nevertheless, they are here and have come in first.
The runners-up are the crocuses.

But the evergreen never went under,
it just spread its branches taut and took the worst
that winter had to offer. Do not go under
and one day you may be crowned with evergreen.
This year is my third spring, the third time
that I have been witness to the cycle of the seasons.

Where I am born, there is no such thing,
seasons just shift over a bit to accommodate
the one following. Our winters bring tangerines
and pimento winds. Bless now death, resurrection,
the peculiar ascension of ice falls finally away.

I think it must be spring now because today
I feel so tender, like all early things budding.
And even if I am coming in exhausted,
bowed, bent, drawn, and yellow-skinned
like my very first quartet of daffodils
I know now that this is undeniably spring.

[Certainties in huge colors]

Certainties in huge colors
like landscapes;
sun without shadows
nothing softer than death.
At night
the eye pierces deeper
and the wind brings back the morning
shivering from full moon
And yet the earth: a vast miracle!

Translated by Elaine Gardiner

[Once, far over the breakers]

Once, far over the breakers,
I caught a glimpse
Of a white bird
And fell in love
With this dream which obsesses me.

Translated by Kenneth Rexroth

Dawn

Does the day break
with the sound of guns?
No,
it breaks with the cry
of that bird
which nibbles through
the night's darkness
very slowly.

Translated by D. N. Bezbarua

I Found It

I found it on a radiant day
after a long drifting.
It was green and blossoming
as the sun over palm trees
scattered golden bouquets;
April was generous that season
with loving and sun.

I found it
after a long wandering.
It was a tender evergreen bough
where birds took shelter,
a bough bending gently under storms
which later was straight again,
rich with sap,
never snapping in the wind's hand.
It stayed supple
as if there were no bad weather,
echoing the brightness of stars,
the gentle breeze,
the dew and the clouds.

I found it
on a vivid summer day
after a long straying,
a tedious search.
It was a quiet lake
where thirsty human wolves
and swirling winds could only briefly
disturb the waters.
Then they would clear again like crystal
to be the moon's mirror,
swimming place of light and blue,
bathing pool for the guardian stars.

I found it!
And now when the storms wail
and the face of the sun is masked in clouds,
when my shining fate revolves to dark,
my light will never be extinguished!
Everything that shadowed my life
wrapping it with night after night
has disappeared, lain down
in memory's grave,
since the day
my soul found
my soul.

Translated by Patricia Alanah Byrne with
the help of Salma al-Khadra' al-Jayyusi
and Naomi Shihab Nye

Anniversary

When the world was created wasn't it like this?

A little flame illuminating a rough sea, a question

of attraction, something fermented, something sweet?

And then a bird or two were added, the crow of course to

joke about humanity, and then another kind so beautiful

we had to hear them first, before our eyes could be
  imagined.

And it was, we were then—and there was no separation.

The cries of a planet formed our becoming.

We peered through the smoke as our shoulders, lips,

emerged from new terrain.

The question mark of creation attracts more questions

until the mind is a spiral of gods strung out way over

our heads, traveling toward the invention of sky.

Move over and let us sleep until the dust settles,

until we can figure this thing out.

What was created next is open to speculation or awe.

The shy fish who had known only water

walked out of the ocean onto dry land,

just like that, to another life.

Frog imagined meals of flying things and creatures in flight
   imagined hills

of daubed dirt and grass in which to settle and make others

to follow in their knowledge which they were building

as sure as houses on the tangled web.

And in that manner we became—elegance of fire, the
   waving grass.

And it's been years.

PART EIGHT

"The Heart Has Found Home"

PEACE TO THE SPIRIT

At the Wall

It is 3:00 A.M. Shabbat.
Our last hour in Jerusalem.
O Jerusalem!
We crawl from the labyrinth
of cobblestones and arches
while cats and rubbish
lurk in narrow alleys.
We slink past soldiers
sleepless and sullen
in their makeshift box
drawn by vagrant dreams
to the Wall.

Under yellow lights it leans,
the old blocks huge
and bruised like human needs.
The empty square rings beneath our feet.
No longer night, nor yet day,
limbo between heaven and earth
claims us. The Wall! The Wall!
A wail of longing in my soul
batters itself against these outsized bricks
and I would wrench prayers from my pride
and press them in paper-stuffed cracks
between my God and me.

Men are here, black clothed
and hatted, and small boys, heads
shaved, ringletted. Women too,
shawled and quiet.
Chastened, I wait
and watch till dawn responds
to murmured hope, the muttering of song,
the heart's chant in the hushed hour.

O, God of Jerusalem, Lord of all
this earth, hear my plea:
Let the wall between Thee and me
melt in mercy, and my praise
raze the rock of thine austerity!

Latter-day Mother Courage

I'm from Latin America,
My land is Argentina,
A latter-day Mother Courage

Of history made black.
Amputated of a son, I pull my sorrows
Without rancor, without hate,

Remembering the eyes of that boy—
So soft, so pure, so handsome.
This is what carries me up the mountainside.

This is what lowers me into the pit of death
Without fear. Because of the flower
With thorns God so beautifully put

In my path, my blood flows
With love
For the children of this land.

If they grow, and if
There are happy mothers,
And if there are many good men,

If they have a free country,
The debt owed to me
Will have been paid.

Translated by Gail Wronsky

Home

Like sapphire and terracotta mingling in the Ganga,
washing the tender limbs of new-borns and the petrified
dead, we live in the melting of colors and continents
as transparent as haze hanging above the river at dawn.

Can the river be holier than the heart, I wonder, here
in the arms of another world, where pain is as clear
as the squeal of a child dipped into winter waters,
more real than corpses floating among white petals.

When the drunk who drags her raggedness on urban streets
moves us as much as the naked children elbowed out
of the golden-domed temple, and when the maple that
    changes,
sheds, and springs again seduces us as much as the jasmine
flowering in torpid heat, then the heart has found home.

[the minute the sun comes out]

the minute the sun comes out

everything is beside the point

it is enough
to open your eyes
to stretch your limbs
like a cat

and all the rest
philosophical
political
systems
deep moral and
aesthetic
disquisitions

are only
a pleasant means of whiling away the time
beautiful baroque flourishes from which you must retreat
to recover
here in the sun
the simple pleasure of your
own
skin

Translated by Thomas Hoeksema

The Forgiveness Dream:
Man from the Warsaw Ghetto

He looked about six or seven, only much too thin.
It seemed right he would be there, but everything,
every lineation, was slow. . . . He was speaking in Polish,
I couldn't answer him.
He pointed at the window, the trees, or the snow,
or our silver auditorium.

I said to him in English, "I've lived the whole time
here, in peace. A private life."   "In shame,"
I said. He nodded. He was old now, kind,
my age, or my mother's age: He nodded,
and wrote in my notebook—"Let it be good."

He frowned, and stopped,
as if he'd forgotten something,
and wrote again,
"Let it."

I walk, and stop, and walk—
touch the birchbark   shining, powdery, cold:
taste the snow, hot on my tongue—
pure cold, licked from the salt of my hand;
This quiet, these still unvisitable stars
move with choices.
Our kin are here.
Were here.

At Gettysburg

These fields can never be
simply themselves. Their green
seems such a tender green,
their contours so significant
to the tourists who stare

towards the far range of mountains
as if they are listening
to the page of history tearing
or to what they know themselves of warfare
between brothers. In this scenery

cows and cannons stand side by side
and motionless, as if they had grown here.
The cannons on their simple wheels
resemble farm carts, children
climb them. Thus function disappears almost entirely

into form, and what is left under
the impartial blue of the sky is a landscape
where dandelions lie in the tall grass
like so many spent cartridges, turning
at last to the smoke

of puffballs; where the only red
visible comes at sunset;
where the earth has grown so lovely
it seems to forgive us even as we are learning
to forgive ourselves.

Now and Then

Slowly, it is dusk,
Morning,
Spring.
Now you notice, now
Believe in what you see.

You always miss that moment
Of things becoming right; the shift's
No sharper than memory's.
Or maybe nothing
Stirs at all,

But the thing you want to fix
Moves through space—fast,
But still, like starlight.
Imagine that you could trap it once
In a mirror balanced between

Now
And then. The mirror, for a moment,
Holds the two apart,
And holds
The parts together.

Lady Spring

Lady Spring
is exquisitely dressed,
enrobed in lemon trees
and orange buds.

Her sandals are wide leaves,
and blushing fuchsias
complete her caravan.

Go out to meet her
along these roads.
She rides with sunshine
and trilled melodies.

Lady Spring,
with luxuriant breath,
laughs at all the world's pains.

She does not believe the one
who tells her about shattered lives.
How can she chance to touch
them among the sweet jasmine?

How can she discover them
reflected in fountains
of looking glass gold
and radiant songs?

From brown cracks
in the sick earth,
rose bushes light up
with red pirouettes.

She puts on her laces,
adorns herself green
over the somber stones
of the dead.

Lady Spring,
with your glorious hands,
make us, in the name of life,
scatter roses:

roses of joy,
roses of forgiveness,
roses of love
and exultation.

Translated by Maria Giachetti

Permissions

"On the Turning Up of Unidentified Black Female Corpses" by Toi Derricotte. From *Captivity*, copyright © 1989 by Toi Derricotte (Pittsburgh, Pa.: University of Pittsburgh Press, 1989). Reprinted by permission of the publisher.

"Infanticide" by Pattiann Rogers. From *Song of the World Becoming: New and Collected Poems, 1981–2001*, copyright © 2001 by Pattiann Rogers (Minneapolis, Minn.: Milkweed Editions, 2001). Reprinted by permission of the publisher.

"Will You Marry Me?" by Taeko Tomioka. From *Other Side River* © 1995 by Leza Lowitz (Berkeley, Ca.: Stone Bridge Press, 1995). Reprinted by permission of the publisher.

"Dearest Love-I" by Salma al-Khadra' al-Jayyusi. From *Women of the Fertile Crescent: Modern Poetry by Arab Women*, edited and copyright © 1981 by Kamal Boullata (Boulder, Co.: Lynne Rienner Publishers, Inc., 1996). Reprinted by permission of the editor.

"Tattoo Writing" by Fawziyya Abu Khalid. From *Women of the Fertile Crescent: Modern Poetry by Arab Women*, edited and copyright © 1981 by Kamal Boullata (Boulder, Co.: Lynne Rienner Publishers, Inc., 1996). Reprinted by permission of the editor.

"Young Wife's Lament" by Brigit Pegeen Kelly. From *To the Place of Trumpets*, copyright © 1988 by Brigit Pegeen Kelly (New Haven, Conn.: Yale University Press, 1988). Reprinted by permission of the publisher.

"If You Think with Fire" by Hsiung Hung. From *Women Poets of China*, translated and copyright © 1973 by Kenneth Rexroth and Ling Chung (New York: New Directions Publishing Corp., 1973). Reprinted by permission of the publisher.

"Woman" by Hira Bansode. From *Oxford Anthology of Modern Indian Poetry*, copyright © 1994 by Vinay Dharwadker and A. K. Ramanujan (Delhi, India: Oxford University Press India, 1994). Reprinted by permission of the publisher.

"Two Women Knitting" by Mrinal Pande. From *Oxford Anthology of Modern Indian Poetry*, copyright © 1994 by Vinay Dharwadker and A. K. Ramanujan (Delhi, India: Oxford University Press India, 1994). Reprinted by permission of the publisher.

"The Gypsy" by Susan Stewart. From *New American Poets of the '90s*, edited and copyright © 1991 by Jack Myers and Roger Weingarten (Boston, Mass.: David R. Godine, 1991). Reprinted by permission of the publisher.

"Weathering Out" by Rita Dove. From *Thomas and Beulah*, copyright © 1986 by Rita Dove (Pittsburgh, Pa.: Carnegie Mellon University Press, 1986). Reprinted by permission of the author.

"Morning Exercises" by Nina Cassian, translated by Andrea Deletant and Brenda Walker. From *Life Sentence: Selected Poems by Nina Cassian*,

Index